CONTENTS

ATOMIC GUIDE for Real Estate

Helping New Home Buyers of India

SUDHIR BHAT

INDIA • SINGAPORE • MALAYSIA

ISBN

Paperback: 979-8-89610-668-5

Hardcase: 979-8-89699-419-0

PREFACE

Roti, Kapda, Aur Makaan (Bread, Clothing, and Housing) – the three fundamental needs of every individual. Among these essential pillars of life, I have dedicated over 25 years of my career to the third necessity: Housing, and more broadly, the field of Real Estate.

Throughout my journey across various verticals of the real estate industry, I have encountered countless individuals investing their life savings without fully understanding where their money was going. Witnessing their plight and helplessness has been deeply troubling. Many of these individuals endured sleepless nights, agonizing over questions: *How will I recover my lifetime savings? What could I have done differently to avoid a bad investment? Whom should I have trusted or avoided?*

These uncertainties often lead to dire consequences, with millions of cases piling up in courts like RERA, NCLT, and Civil Courts. I have seen heart-wrenching stories of customers losing their dream homes—some even passing away before realizing their aspirations. I have watched young couples who invested in their ideal homes grow old, waiting endlessly for a place where they hoped their children could thrive amidst promised amenities.

These experiences left a deep impression on me and instilled a desire to make a difference. I wanted to empower prospective homebuyers with the knowledge to make informed decisions and avoid the pitfalls that have ensnared so many others. This desire inspired me to write this book.

In creating this guide, I have drawn from a wealth of resources—books on investment and real estate, articles published in newspapers, and insights shared on various platforms. Most importantly, I have infused it with the knowledge and understanding accumulated during my career in the real estate sector.

If this book helps even a single homebuyer avoid a poor investment, achieve their dream home, or make a well-informed decision, I will consider the purpose of this book fulfilled. My hope is that this guide becomes a beacon for anyone embarking on the significant journey of buying their home, equipping them with the tools and confidence to navigate the complexities of the process.

Your dream home is more than just a house—it's a foundation for your future. Let this book be your trusted guide.

INTRODUCTION

Why Buy A Home?

- Here are several compelling reasons why buying a home can be a beneficial decision:

1. **Building Equity and Wealth**

   - **Equity Growth:** Every mortgage payment you make reduces your loan balance, gradually increasing your ownership stake in the property. Over time, as you pay down your mortgage and property values potentially increase, your equity builds, contributing to your overall net worth.

   - **Wealth Accumulation:** Unlike renting, where payments provide no return, homeownership offers the potential for long-term wealth accumulation. Many people view real estate as a cornerstone of their financial planning, with the potential for significant appreciation over time.

2. **Stability and Control**

   - **Predictable Costs:** With a fixed-rate mortgage, your monthly payments remain consistent, unlike rent, which may increase annually. This stability makes it easier to budget for housing expenses over the long term.

   - **Freedom to Personalize:** Owning your home gives you the freedom to customize and renovate the property as you see fit. From painting walls to major renovations, you have full control over your living space, which isn't possible in most rental situations.

3. Tax Benefits

- **Mortgage Interest Deduction:** Homeowners can often deduct mortgage interest payments on their income tax returns, which can result in significant savings, especially in the early years of a mortgage when interest payments are highest.

4. Forced Savings Mechanism

- **Regular Mortgage Payments as Savings:** Paying down a mortgage each month acts like a forced savings plan. It ensures you're investing a portion of your income into a valuable asset, rather than spending it on rent with no return.

5. Appreciation Potential

- **Market Appreciation:** Historically, real estate tends to appreciate over time. While there are fluctuations, many people see their homes increase in value, offering the potential for significant returns when they choose to sell.

- **Neighbourhood Development:** Investing in an up-and-coming area can yield even greater appreciation potential. Researching market trends and developments can help identify properties with high growth prospects.

6. Personal Satisfaction and Comfort

- **Sense of Accomplishment:** Owning a home often represents a major life milestone and source of personal pride. It provides a sense of achievement and belonging in a community.

- **Privacy and Security:** Homeownership often provides a greater sense of privacy and security compared to renting. You have control over your environment, your neighbour's, and the ability to create a space that truly feels like home.

7. Protection Against Inflation

- **Fixed-Rate EMI Advantage:** With inflation, the cost of goods and services tends to rise. However, with a fixed EMI's, your housing costs remain stable, effectively protecting you from inflationary pressures. Meanwhile, rental prices may increase over time, often faster than inflation.

8. Community Engagement and Stability

- **Deeper Community Ties:** Homeowners often feel more connected to their communities. They tend to stay in one place longer, develop relationships with neighbours, and engage more in local activities and organizations.

- **School Stability:** For families, homeownership can provide stability in school districts, which is important for children's education and social development.

9. Leveraging Investment Opportunities

- **Using Leverage:** Real estate allows you to leverage a relatively small amount of money (your down payment) to control a much larger asset. This leverage can multiply your returns on investment, especially in a growing market.

10. Emotional Security

- **Long-Term Roots:** Owning a home provides a sense of permanence and roots in a community, which can be emotionally fulfilling. It offers a stable environment for families to grow and build memories.

Summary

Buying a home can offer financial advantages, emotional satisfaction, and stability that renting often lacks. It's a significant investment, but with careful planning and understanding, it can be a key step toward building long-term wealth and achieving personal goals.

Common Fears and Misconceptions of First-Time Buyers

First-time homebuyers often have several fears and misconceptions that can create anxiety or prevent them from taking the plunge into homeownership. Understanding and addressing these concerns can help alleviate the stress and confusion many new buyers face.

1. Fear of Not Being Able to Afford a Home

- **Misconception:** "I can't afford to buy a home because I need a huge down payment."
  - ♦ **Reality:** While a 20% down payment is ideal, it is not always necessary. Many loan programs, also help the first time buyers to finance their earnest money.

2. Fear of Hidden Costs and Unforeseen Expenses

- **Misconception:** "Owning a home is too expensive because of all the hidden costs."
  - ♦ **Reality:** While there are additional expenses such as property taxes, insurance, maintenance, and closing costs, these can be planned for and managed with proper budgeting. Unlike rent, mortgage payments can build equity over time, making these costs an investment rather than an expense.

3. Fear of the Mortgage Process

- **Misconception:** "Getting a mortgage is complicated and requires perfect credit."
  - ♦ **Reality:** The mortgage process can be complex, but there are professionals (like mortgage brokers and real estate agents) who can help navigate it. While having good credit can improve loan terms, many lenders offer programs for those with less-than-perfect credit.

4. Fear of Overpaying or Buying at the Wrong Time

- **Misconception:** "I will buy at the wrong time and overpay for the property."
  - ♦ **Reality:** The real estate market does fluctuate, but trying to time the market perfectly is almost impossible. The best time

to buy is when you are financially ready and find a home that meets your needs and budget. Over time, property values generally increase, making it a long-term investment.

5. Fear of Making a Poor Investment

- **Misconception:** "What if I buy a house and its value drops?"
    - ♦ **Reality:** While market fluctuations can occur, real estate historically appreciates over the long term. The risk of value depreciation is rear when you buy in a good location, maintain the property, and plan to stay for several years.

6. Fear of Committing to One Location

- **Misconception:** "Owning a home ties me down, and I won't be able to move."
    - ♦ **Reality:** While buying a home is a commitment, it doesn't mean you're stuck forever. If circumstances change, you can always rent out the property or sell it. Additionally, owning a home can provide more financial flexibility to make future moves.

7. Fear of Maintenance and Repairs

- **Misconception:** "I'll have to handle all repairs and maintenance myself, and it will be overwhelming."
    - ♦ **Reality:** While homeowners are responsible for repairs, many of these can be managed with a home warranty or by budgeting a small amount each month for upkeep. Routine maintenance helps prevent bigger, more costly repairs down the line.

8. Misunderstanding of Homeownership Responsibilities

- **Misconception:** "I won't have the time or knowledge to manage a home."
    - ♦ **Reality:** Homeownership does come with new responsibilities, but many resources and professionals (e.g., real estate agents, Lenders, Sales Person) are available to help. Home maintenance skills can also be learned over time, and some tasks can be outsourced to professionals.

9. Fear of Getting Stuck in a Bad Deal

- **Misconception:** "I'm afraid of buying a home with hidden issues or getting scammed."

  - **Reality:** Professional home inspections and due diligence can uncover potential problems before closing. A reputable real estate agent and a good lawyer can also protect you from making a poor deal.

10. Fear of the Unknown

- **Misconception:** "The home-buying process is too complicated, and I don't know where to start."

  - **Reality:** The process can feel overwhelming, but it is manageable when broken down into steps. Education, guidance from real estate professionals, and using resources like first-time homebuyer programs can simplify the process.

11. Belief that Renting is Always Cheaper

- **Misconception:** "Renting is always cheaper and less risky than buying."

  - **Reality:** While renting may seem cheaper in the short term, buying a home can be more cost-effective over time due to building equity, tax benefits, and the potential for property value appreciation. Rent also tends to increase over time, while a fixed EMI's remains stable.

12. Fear of Losing Job or Financial Stability

- **Misconception:** "If I lose my job or my financial situation changes, I could lose my home."

  - **Reality:** While financial stability is important, emergency funds and other safety nets (like mortgage protection insurance) can provide a buffer. Additionally, options like refinancing or negotiating with your lender can provide relief during difficult times.

13. Fear of the Length of Mortgage Commitment

- **Misconception:** "A 20-year mortgage is a lifetime commitment, and that's too long."

    - **Reality:** While a mortgage term is often long, you don't have to keep the mortgage for its full duration. Many homeowners sell, refinance, or pay off their mortgages early, giving them more flexibility than they initially expect.

Summary

Understanding these fears and misconceptions is the first step toward overcoming them. Homeownership is a significant decision, but with the right information, preparation, and professional guidance, it can be a rewarding and financially beneficial experience.

What You Will Learn from This Book

1. Step-by-Step Guidance on the Home Buying Process

- **Clear Understanding of the Entire Home Buying Journey:** Learn every step of the home buying process, from initial planning to closing the deal, with a structured roadmap designed for first-time buyers.

- **Roles of Key Players:** Understand the roles of real estate agents, lenders, inspectors, and lawyers, and how to work with them effectively.

2. Financial Preparation and Budgeting for Your First Home

- **Assessing Your Financial Health:** Learn how to evaluate your financial situation, including calculating how much home you can afford, understanding your credit score, and developing a down payment strategy.

- **Exploring Financing Options:** Discover various mortgage types and how to choose the right one for your situation. Understand fixed vs. variable rates and the benefits of getting pre-approved for a loan.

- **Understanding Hidden Costs:** Learn about the costs associated with buying a home, such as closing costs, property taxes, and maintenance expenses, and how to budget for them.

3. Strategies for Finding and Choosing the Right Home

- **Defining Your Home Criteria:** Learn how to identify your needs vs. wants, assess different types of properties, and choose the best location for your lifestyle and investment goals.

- **Conducting an Effective Home Search:** Master the art of finding properties, using online tools, attending open houses, and working with real estate agents. Learn how to evaluate potential homes, recognizing both red flags and positive attributes.

4. Mastering the Art of Making Offers and Negotiations

- **Making a Competitive Offer:** Gain insights into how to craft a strong offer, understand market dynamics, and determine the right price for a home.

- **Negotiation Tactics:** Learn how to handle counteroffers, negotiate contingencies, and know when to walk away from a deal that doesn't meet your needs.

5. Navigating Inspections, Appraisals, and Legal Requirements

- **Understanding Home Inspections and Appraisals:** Learn what to expect during a home inspection, how to select a reputable inspector, and how to deal with any issues that arise. Understand the appraisal process and its impact on your mortgage.

- **Legal Aspects of Buying a Home:** Gain knowledge of key legal documents, contracts, and contingencies, and how to protect your interests throughout the buying process.

6. Closing the Deal and Transitioning to Homeownership

- **Preparing for Closing Day:** Learn what happens during closing, including a breakdown of closing costs, required documents, and the final walkthrough.

- **Securing Your Financing:** Understand the steps to finalize your mortgage, including reviewing loan terms and understanding your rights and responsibilities.

- **Moving In and Settling Down:** Get practical tips for planning your move, setting up utilities, and creating a comfortable home environment.

7. Managing Life as a Homeowner

- **Budgeting for Homeownership:** Learn how to manage monthly expenses, save for maintenance and repairs, and build an emergency fund.

- **Building Equity and Long-Term Value:** Understand how to build equity over time, improve your home's value through smart upgrades, and make informed decisions about refinancing or selling.

- **Home Maintenance and Care:** Learn basic home maintenance tips and how to handle common repairs, ensuring your property remains in good condition.

8. Overcoming Common Fears and Misconceptions

- **Addressing First-Time Buyer Concerns:** Gain confidence by dispelling myths and understanding the realities of buying a home, from affordability and market timing to maintenance and long-term commitment.

9. Leveraging Resources and Support Systems

- **Utilizing Available Resources:** Discover government programs, grants, and incentives designed for first-time homebuyers, as well as tips on finding reliable real estate professionals and support networks.

- **Accessing Checklists, Tools, and Templates:** Benefit from practical tools, checklists, and templates that simplify the home buying process and help you stay organized.

10. Building Confidence for Future Real Estate Decisions

- **Laying the Foundation for Future Investments:** Learn how this first purchase can be a stepping stone to future real estate investments, setting the stage for building wealth and financial security.

Summary

By the end of the book, you will feel empowered with the knowledge, confidence, and tools needed to navigate the home buying process successfully, make informed decisions, and achieve your dream of homeownership.

PART 1

PREPARING FOR HOME OWNERSHIP

CHAPTER 1

UNDERSTANDING THE HOME BUYING PROCESS

Step 1: Assess Your Financial Situation

- **Evaluate Your Finances:** Review your income, expenses, savings, and debts to determine how much you can afford to spend on a home.

- **Check Your Credit Score:** Understand your credit score and history, as these will impact your ability to secure a mortgage and the interest rate you'll be offered.

- **Create a Budget:** Outline a budget for your home purchase, including the down payment, closing costs, and ongoing homeownership expenses like property taxes, insurance, and maintenance.

Step 2: Determine Your Home Loan Eligibility

- **Research Home Loan Options:** Compare home loan offerings from various banks and financial institutions. Look at interest rates, tenure, processing fees, and terms and conditions.

- **Check Eligibility Criteria:** Use online calculators to check your eligibility based on your income, age, employment status, and credit history.

- **Get Pre-Approved for a Loan:** Obtain a pre-approval letter from the bank, which helps you understand your maximum loan amount and shows sellers that you are a serious buyer.

Step 3: Decide the Location and Type of Property

- **Choose the Right Location:** Research locations that suit your lifestyle, work, and family needs. Consider factors like proximity to schools, workplaces, hospitals, transportation, and other amenities.

- **Select the Type of Property:** Decide whether you want an apartment, villa, independent house, or plot. Consider the size, layout, and facilities offered by different types of properties.

- **Assess the Real Estate Market:** Study market trends, price appreciation potential, and any upcoming infrastructure developments in your chosen location.

Step 4: Start the Property Search

- **Hire a Real Estate Agent (Optional):** Consider hiring a local real estate agent who has expertise in the area you are interested in. They can provide valuable insights and help identify properties that meet your criteria.

- **Explore Online and Offline Listings:** Use property portals, social media, classifieds, and real estate websites to find listings. Also, visit real estate fairs and exhibitions

- **Shortlist Properties:** Narrow down your options based on your budget, preferences, and the property's legal status.

Step 5: Verify the Property's Legal Status

- **Conduct a Title Search:** Verify the title of the property to ensure it is clear of any encumbrances or disputes. Check that the seller has the legal right to sell the property.

- **Check Required Approvals:** Ensure the property has the necessary approvals from local authorities, such as building permits, environmental clearances, and municipal approvals.

- **Confirm Property Documents:** Review documents like the Sale Deed, Mother Deed, Encumbrance Certificate, Occupancy Certificate, Khata Certificate, and NOCs from relevant authorities.

Step 6: Make an Offer and Negotiate the Price

- **Make an Offer:** Once you find a suitable property, make a formal offer to the seller, either directly or through your agent.

- **Negotiate Terms and Conditions:** Negotiate the price, payment schedule, possession date, and any additional terms or conditions with the seller.

- **Draft a Sale Agreement:** Prepare a Sale Agreement, outlining the agreed-upon terms, which both parties will sign. This document typically includes a token amount or earnest money to secure the deal.

Step 7: Apply for Home Loan

- **Submit a Loan Application:** Apply for a home loan with your chosen bank or financial institution, providing all required documentation (e.g., income proof, identity proof, property documents).

- **Loan Processing and Sanction:** The bank will conduct a legal check of the property, verify your documents, and perform a technical evaluation of the property. Once satisfied, they will sanction the loan amount.

- **Sign the Loan Agreement:** After the loan is approved, you must sign the loan agreement and complete the necessary formalities to disburse the loan amount

Step 8: Execute the Sale Deed and Register the Property

- **Draft the Sale Deed:** Prepare the Sale Deed, a legally binding document outlining the transfer of property ownership from the seller to the buyer. Ensure all details are accurate and that the deed is executed on stamp paper of requisite value.

- **Pay Stamp Duty and Registration Charges:** Pay the stamp duty, registration charges, and other applicable fees to the local sub-registrar's office. The amount varies depending on the property's location and value.

- **Register the Sale Deed:** Both parties must visit the sub-registrar's office to register the Sale Deed. You must bring all necessary documents, including ID proof, photographs, and witnesses

Step 9: Take Possession of the Property

- **Obtain Possession Letter:** Once the registration is complete and all payments are made, obtain a Possession Letter from the seller. This document officially transfers possession of the property to you.

- **Handover of Property Documents:** Ensure that all original property documents, keys, and other relevant papers are handed over to you by the seller.

- **Verify Utility Connections:** Check and transfer utilities (water, electricity, gas, etc.) to your name and ensure they are in working order.

Step 10: Update Records and Pay Taxes

- **Apply for Mutation of Property:** Apply for the mutation of the property in the local municipal records to update ownership details and ensure property tax bills are generated in your name.

- **Pay Property Taxes:** Start paying property taxes to the local municipal authority as the new owner.

Summary

Buying a home in India involves several steps, including financial planning, choosing the right property, verifying legal documents, obtaining financing, and completing the registration process. Each step is crucial to ensuring a smooth transaction and safeguarding your investment.

Key Players: Involved in Home Buying Process

1. Homebuyer

- **Role:** The primary individual or individuals purchasing the property. Homebuyers need to define their needs, conduct thorough research, arrange financing, and coordinate with all other key players throughout the process.

- **Responsibilities:** Assessing financial readiness, selecting the property, negotiating the price and terms, securing a home loan, ensuring legal compliance, and closing the deal.

2. Real Estate Agent / Broker

- **Role:** A professional who assists the buyer in finding a suitable property. They have in-depth knowledge of the local market, property values, and legal requirements. They often act as intermediaries between buyers and sellers.

- **Responsibilities:** Understanding the buyer's requirements, identifying and shortlisting properties, arranging property visits, negotiating the price and terms, and helping with paperwork and legal documentation.

3. Seller (Property Owner)

- **Role:** The current owner of the property who wants to sell it. They could be an individual, a developer, or a real estate investor.

- **Responsibilities:** Providing all necessary property documents, negotiating with potential buyers, and completing the sale according to the terms agreed upon.

4. Lender (Bank or Financial Institution)

- **Role:** The entity that provides the home loan or mortgage to the buyer. Lenders play a crucial role in the home-buying process by assessing the buyer's financial eligibility and determining the loan amount, interest rate, and repayment terms.

- **Responsibilities:** Conducting credit checks, processing the loan application, conducting a property appraisal, sanctioning and disbursing the loan, and managing the loan repayment process.

5. Lawyer / Legal Advisor

- **Role:** A professional who provides legal assistance throughout the home-buying process. They help ensure that all property documents are in order and the transaction complies with all applicable laws.

- **Responsibilities:** Conducting a title search, verifying the property's legal status, preparing or reviewing the Sale Agreement and Sale Deed, assisting with registration, and addressing any legal disputes or issues.

6. Home Inspector / Property Valuer

- **Role:** A qualified professional who evaluates the property's condition and market value. A home inspector examines the physical condition, while a property valuer assesses the market value.

- **Responsibilities:**
  - **Home Inspector:** Checking the property for structural issues, pest infestations, electrical and plumbing problems, and overall maintenance status. Providing a detailed inspection report to the buyer.
  - **Property Valuer:** Assessing the market value of the property, which helps in loan approval and negotiation of the purchase price.

7. Developer / Builder

- **Role:** The entity that constructs residential properties (apartments, villas, etc.) for sale. Developers are crucial players, especially when buying new or under-construction properties.

- **Responsibilities:** Developing the property, obtaining necessary approvals and clearances, selling the property, providing possession, and handling warranties and after-sales service.

8. Local Authorities and Government Bodies

- **Role:** Regulatory bodies and authorities involved in approving and registering the property. They ensure compliance with local laws and regulations.

- **Responsibilities:**
  - ◆ **Municipal Corporation / Local Authority:** Providing approvals for construction, issuing Occupancy Certificates (OC), handling property tax records, and processing property mutations.
  - ◆ **Sub-Registrar's Office:** Responsible for registering the Sale Deed and ensuring the legality of the property transaction.
  - ◆ **RERA (Real Estate Regulatory Authority):** Ensuring that developers and real estate agents comply with the Real Estate (Regulation and Development) Act, 2016, protecting buyer interests.

9. Chartered Accountant (CA)

- **Role:** A financial advisor who provides tax-related advice and assistance in managing financial aspects of the transaction, such as verifying tax liabilities, capital gains, and other financial implications.
- **Responsibilities:** Advising on tax benefits related to home loans, calculating property tax liabilities, assisting in tax planning, and guiding the buyer through financial documentation.

10. Notary

- **Role:** A licensed legal professional who verifies and notarizes documents to authenticate their validity.
- **Responsibilities:** Notarizing property documents such as Power of Attorney, affidavits, and agreements to ensure their legal authenticity.

11. Mortgage Broker (Optional)

- **Role:** A professional who helps buyers find and secure a home loan from different lenders by comparing interest rates and terms.
- **Responsibilities:** Assisting the buyer in choosing the right loan, negotiating with lenders, completing loan applications, and guiding through the loan approval process.

12. Insurance Provider

- **Role:** The entity that offers property insurance, home loan insurance, and other relevant insurance policies to protect the buyer's investment.

- **Responsibilities:** Providing home insurance to cover potential damages or losses and loan insurance to cover outstanding loans in case of unforeseen circumstances.

13. Society / Resident Welfare Association (RWA) (for Apartments)

- **Role:** The governing body that manages the maintenance and administration of a housing society or apartment complex.

- **Responsibilities:** Providing a No Objection Certificate (NOC) for the sale, verifying the buyer's credentials, and ensuring compliance with society rules and regulations.

14. Home Loan Insurance Provider (Optional)

- **Role:** An insurance provider offering loan protection plans that cover the outstanding loan amount in case of the borrower's death or disability.

- **Responsibilities:** Providing loan insurance policies to protect the lender and borrower from unforeseen circumstances that may affect loan repayment.

Summary

The home-buying process in India involves coordination among various key players, each with a distinct role and set of responsibilities. Understanding their roles helps buyers navigate the complex process, ensuring a smooth and legally compliant transaction.

CHAPTER 2

FINANCIAL PREPARATION

Assessing Your Financial Health

Assessing your financial health is a crucial first step in the home-buying process in India. It helps you determine how much you can afford, your eligibility for a home loan, and the overall feasibility of buying a home. Here's a comprehensive guide to evaluating your financial health:

1. Calculate Your Net Worth

- **List Your Assets:** Calculate the total value of your assets, including savings, fixed deposits, mutual funds, stocks, retirement funds, jewellery, and existing real estate or other investments.

- **List Your Liabilities:** Identify all your liabilities, such as outstanding loans (personal loans, car loans, credit card debt), mortgages, and any other debts.

- **Determine Your Net Worth:** Subtract your total liabilities from your total assets to determine your net worth. A positive net worth indicates a healthy financial position.

  - **Total Assets Value – Total Liabilities Value = Net Worth of Individual**

2. Evaluate Your Monthly Income and Expenses

- **Calculate Your Monthly Income:** Include all sources of income such as salary, rental income, business income, freelance work, investments (dividends, interest), and any other recurring income.

- **Track Your Monthly Expenses:** Record all monthly expenses, including fixed expenses (rent, EMIs, insurance premiums), variable expenses (groceries, utilities, transportation), and discretionary spending (entertainment, dining out).

- **Calculate Your Surplus:** Subtract total monthly expenses from your monthly income to determine your surplus. This surplus will indicate how much you can save or allocate towards a home purchase.

  - ➢ **Total Monthly Income – Total Monthly Expenses = Surplus per month**

3. Review Your Credit Score and Report

- **Check Your Credit Score:** Obtain your credit score from a credit bureau like CIBIL, Equifax, or Experian. In India, a CIBIL score of 750 or above is considered good for securing a home loan at favourable terms.

- **Analyse Your Credit Report:** Review your credit report to check for any discrepancies, unpaid dues, or errors that could impact your creditworthiness. Rectify any issues before applying for a loan.

- **Improve Your Credit Score:** If your score is low, work on improving it by paying off existing debts, avoiding late payments, and reducing credit card utilization.

4. Determine Your Home Affordability

- **Use the 28/36 Rule:** Financial experts suggest spending no more than 28% of your gross monthly income on housing costs (EMI, property taxes, and insurance) and no more than 36% on total debt obligations (including housing costs, credit card payments, and other loans).

- **Calculate the Maximum EMI You Can Afford:** Based on your income and expenses, determine the maximum monthly EMI you can afford comfortably. This amount will help you understand your loan eligibility.

- **Decide on the Down Payment:** Most lenders in India require a down payment of at least 10-20% of the property's value. Ensure you have sufficient savings for the down payment, along with extra funds for registration, stamp duty, and other costs. However if you are entitled for more than the loan that you require, same can be paid by the lender only but depends on person to person financial health.

5. Analyse Your Debt-to-Income (DTI) Ratio

- **Calculate Your DTI Ratio:** Divide your total monthly debt payments (including the new EMI) by your gross monthly income. The lower the DTI ratio, the better your chances of securing a loan. Aim for a DTI ratio of 40% or less.

- **Understand the Impact on Loan Eligibility:** A higher DTI ratio might limit your loan eligibility or result in higher interest rates. Reduce existing debt to lower your DTI ratio.

6. Build an Emergency Fund

- **Create an Emergency Fund:** Ensure you have an emergency fund equivalent to at least 6-12 months of living expenses. This fund should cover your EMIs, household expenses, and other financial obligations in case of a job loss or unexpected event.

- **Keep Liquid Assets:** Maintain sufficient liquid assets (cash, savings, liquid mutual funds) that can be easily accessed during emergencies without selling long-term investments.

7. Assess Additional Costs of Homeownership

- **Factor in Property-Related Costs:** Beyond the property's purchase price, account for additional costs such as stamp duty, registration fees, legal fees, property taxes, home insurance, and maintenance charges.

- **Consider Home Furnishing and Moving Costs:** Plan for expenses related to moving, furnishing, and setting up your new home (e.g., appliances, furniture, and interior decoration).

- **Prepare for Ongoing Maintenance Costs:** Account for ongoing maintenance, utility bills, repairs, and other regular expenses.

8. Plan for Tax Benefits and Savings

- **Understand Tax Benefits on Home Loans:** In India, you can claim tax deductions on home loan interest payments under Section 24(b) and on principal repayment under Section 80C of the Income Tax Act. These benefits can significantly reduce your tax liability.

- **Consult a Tax Advisor:** A tax advisor can help you understand the exact benefits available and guide you on optimizing your tax savings while purchasing a home.

9. Evaluate Your Investment and Retirement Goals

- **Align Home Purchase with Financial Goals:** Ensure that buying a home aligns with your other financial goals, such as children's education, retirement planning, or other major life events.

- **Review Your Investment Portfolio:** Assess whether buying a home will impact your ability to save for other long-term goals. Avoid liquidating investments that are earmarked for other critical objectives.

10. Plan for Future Financial Commitments

- **Consider Future Financial Obligations:** Assess any upcoming expenses like marriage, education, or business investments, and plan how buying a home will impact these commitments.

- **Plan for Rate Fluctuations:** Understand that home loan interest rates in India are often variable. Ensure you have a buffer in your budget to accommodate potential rate increases.

Summary of Steps for Assessing Financial Health

1. Calculate Your Net Worth
2. Evaluate Your Monthly Income and Expenses
3. Review Your Credit Score and Report
4. Determine Your Home Affordability
5. Analyse Your Debt-to-Income (DTI) Ratio
6. Build an Emergency Fund
7. Assess Additional Costs of Homeownership
8. Plan for Tax Benefits and Savings
9. Evaluate Your Investment and Retirement Goals
10. Plan for Future Financial Commitments

By thoroughly assessing your financial health, you can make informed decisions about the type of property you can afford, the loan amount you qualify for, and the overall feasibility of your home purchase in India.

CALCULATE HOW MUCH YOU CAN AFFORD

Calculating how much home you can afford in India involves understanding your budget constraints, financial goals, and the costs associated with purchasing and maintaining a property. Here is a step-by-step guide to determining the maximum home price you can comfortably afford:

1. Calculate Your Monthly Income

- **Determine Gross Monthly Income:** Include all sources of income, such as salary, bonuses, rental income, business income, freelance work, interest, and dividends.

- **Include Joint Income (if applicable):** If you are purchasing a home with a spouse or family member, include their income as well, since it may increase your eligibility for a higher loan amount.

2. Understand the 28/36 Rule

The **28/36 Rule** is a common guideline used to determine home affordability:

- **28% Rule:** Spend no more than 28% of your gross monthly income on housing costs (including the home loan EMI, property taxes, and insurance).

- **36% Rule:** Ensure that total monthly debt payments, including the new home loan EMI and other debts (e.g., car loans, personal loans, credit card debt), do not exceed 36% of your gross monthly income.

3. Calculate Your Monthly Housing Budget

- **Monthly Housing Budget Formula:** Maximum Monthly Housing Budget = Gross Monthly Income×0.28

- For example, if your gross monthly income is ₹1,00,000, the maximum amount you should spend on housing costs is: Maximum Monthly Housing Budget = 1,00,000×0.28=₹28,000.00

4. Determine Your Loan Eligibility

- **Use the Loan-to-Value (LTV) Ratio:** In India, lenders typically offer up to 75-90% of the property's value as a loan. The remaining 10-25% needs to be paid as a down payment.

- **Calculate Loan Amount Based on EMI Affordability:**
  - ♦ Lenders use your monthly income, existing liabilities, and credit score to determine the maximum EMI you can afford.

    A common formula is:

    Loan Amount = ((1+Interest Rate)n–1Affordable EMI×(1+Interest Rate)n

  - ♦ **n** is the loan tenure in months (e.g., 20 years = 240 months).
  - ♦ $1/(1+r)^1 + 1/(1+r)^2 + + 1/(1+r)^3\dots\dots\dots\dots\dots+ 1/(1+r)^n$

Example Calculation:

- **Assumptions:**
  - ♦ Affordable EMI: ₹28,000
  - ♦ Interest Rate: 7% per annum (0.583% per month)
  - ♦ Loan Tenure: 20 years (240 months)
  - ♦ Calculate the approximate loan amount you may be eligible for based on these factors.
  - ♦ **Loan Amount** = 28000 X 128.98

    (Sum total of Interest Rate for 240 Months)

    $$= Rs.36,11,440/-$$

- Formula to Calculate EMI on Loans

  $P \times R \times (1+R)^N / [(1+R)^{N-1}]$

  P: Principal Loan Amount = INR 10,00,000/-

  N: Loan Tenure in Months = 10 Yrs = 120 Months

  R: Interest Rate / Month = 7.2% = 7.2/12/100 = 0.006

  $EMI = 10,00,000 \times 0.006 \times (1+0.006)^{120} / ((1+0.006)^{120-1})$
  $$= Rs.11,714$$

5. Estimate the Down Payment

- **Calculate Minimum Down Payment:**

  Determine the down payment amount required, typically 10-25% of the property value. For example,

  if the property is valued at ₹50,00,000, and the bank requires a 20% down payment:

  Down Payment=50,00,000×0.20=₹10,00,000

Consider Savings for Down Payment: Ensure that you have sufficient savings for the down payment without compromising your emergency fund or other critical financial goals.

6. Account for Additional Costs

- **Registration and Stamp Duty:** Include costs for stamp duty (typically 5-8% of the property value, depending on the state) and registration fees (around 1-2% of the property value).

- **Legal Fees and Due Diligence:** Set aside funds for hiring a lawyer, verifying documents, and other legal formalities.

- **Home Insurance:** Estimate the cost of home insurance, which protects your investment against natural disasters, theft, or damages.

- **Furnishing and Moving Costs:** Plan for additional expenses related to moving, furnishing, or renovating the home.

7. Consider Tax Benefits on Home Loans

- **Understand Tax Deductions:** The Income Tax Act, 1961, allows tax benefits on both the principal repayment (up to ₹1.5 lakh under Section 80C) and interest payment (up to ₹2 lakh under Section 24(b)) of a home loan. These deductions can lower your overall tax liability and make the loan more affordable.

- **Factor in Tax Savings:** Calculate the potential tax savings to understand how it impacts your net outflow.

8. Use a Home Affordability Calculator

- **Online Calculators:** Use an online home affordability calculator, which considers factors such as income, expenses, interest rate, loan tenure, and existing liabilities. Input your details to get a quick estimate of how much home you can afford.

9. Align with Your Long-Term Financial Goals

- **Review Future Financial Goals:** Ensure that buying a home does not compromise other financial goals, such as retirement savings, children's education, or emergency funds.

- **Plan for Rate Fluctuations:** Keep a buffer in your budget to accommodate potential increases in loan interest rates over time.

10. Arrive at the Final Budget

- **Determine Your Final Budget:** Combine the EMI you can comfortably afford with the down payment and additional costs to determine the maximum home price you can afford.

- **Prioritize Comfort Over Stretching:** Choose a property that fits well within your budget to avoid financial stress and maintain a healthy lifestyle.

Example of Affordability Calculation:

1. **Gross Monthly Income:** ₹1,00,000
2. **Maximum Monthly Housing Budget (28% of Income):** ₹28,000
3. **Assumed Home Loan Interest Rate:** 7% per annum
4. **Loan Tenure:** 20 years (240 months)
5. **Estimated Loan Eligibility (based on EMI):** Approximately ₹40-45 lakh
6. **Down Payment (20% of ₹50 lakh property):** ₹10 lakh
7. **Additional Costs (Stamp Duty, Registration, etc.):** ₹3-5 lakh

Summary

- **Total Home Price You Can Afford:** Approximately ₹50 lakh

- **Home Loan Amount:** ₹40 lakh

- **Down Payment and Other Costs:** ₹13-15 lakh

- By following these steps, you can arrive at a realistic budget for buying a home in India while ensuring that the purchase aligns with your financial situation and long-term goals.

BUILDING A DOWNPAYMENT AND SAVING STRATEGY

Building a down payment and savings strategy is a key step toward buying a home in India. Since most lenders require a down payment of 10-25% of the property's value, having a solid plan to save for this amount is essential. Here's a comprehensive guide to help you develop a strategy to build your down payment and grow your savings effectively.

1. Determine Your Down Payment Amount

- **Estimate the Property Price:** Identify the approximate value of the property you want to buy. For example, if you are looking at properties worth ₹50 lakhs, this is your target amount.

- **Calculate the Required Down Payment:** In India, banks typically require a down payment of 10-25% of the property value.

- If the property costs ₹50 lakhs and the bank requires a 20% down payment: Down Payment=50,00,000×0.20=₹10,00,000

2. Set a Savings Goal and Timeline

- **Determine Your Timeline:** Decide by when you want to purchase your home. For example, if you plan to buy a home in 3 years, this is your timeline.

- **Calculate Monthly Savings Needed:** Divide the down payment amount by the number of months available to save.

- If you need ₹10,00,000.00 in 3 years (36 months): Monthly Savings Required=₹10,00,000.00/36= ₹27,778

- **Adjust for Inflation:** Consider inflation and property price appreciation, and aim to save 5-10% more than your initial goal.

3. Evaluate Your Current Financial Situation

- **Assess Your Current Savings:** Review your existing savings, investments, and assets that can be allocated toward the down payment.

- **Analyse Your Monthly Budget:** Identify areas where you can cut costs or reduce discretionary spending to increase your savings rate.

- **Pay Off High-Interest Debt:** Prioritize paying off high-interest debt (e.g., credit card debt, personal loans) before building your down payment, as these can hinder your savings potential.

4. Create a Dedicated Savings Account

- **Open a Separate Savings Account:** Create a dedicated savings account specifically for your down payment to avoid mixing funds and ensure discipline.

- **Opt for High-Interest Savings Accounts:** Choose a high-interest savings account or a fixed deposit (FD) that offers competitive interest rates to maximize your returns.

5. Automate Your Savings

- **Set Up Automatic Transfers:** Automate monthly transfers from your salary account to your dedicated down payment savings account. This ensures consistent savings without the temptation to spend.

- **Use Savings Apps and Tools:** Use mobile banking apps or budgeting tools to set savings goals, track progress, and receive reminders.

6. Explore Investment Options to Grow Savings

- **Fixed Deposits (FDs):** FDs are low-risk and offer fixed returns, making them ideal for short-term savings (1-3 years). Compare FD rates across banks and choose one with the highest returns.

- **Recurring Deposits (RDs):** RDs allow you to save a fixed amount every month for a specified tenure, providing compounded interest. This is a good option for disciplined savings.

- **Mutual Funds (Short-Term Debt Funds):** Consider investing in short-term debt mutual funds or liquid funds, which offer better returns than savings accounts and are relatively low-risk.

- **Systematic Investment Plan (SIP):** If you have a longer time horizon (3-5 years), consider SIPs in balanced or conservative mutual funds to benefit from market-linked returns.

- **Public Provident Fund (PPF):** PPF offers tax-free returns and is a good option for long-term savings (15 years). However, it has a lock-in period, so it's suitable for those who plan to buy a home in the long term.

7. Cut Down on Non-Essential Expenses

- **Track Your Spending:** Identify non-essential expenses (e.g., dining out, subscriptions, entertainment) and cut back where possible.

- **Adopt a Frugal Lifestyle:** Make small lifestyle changes, such as cooking at home, carpooling, or using public transport, to save more.

- **Review and Optimize Monthly Bills:** Negotiate better rates for utilities, insurance, internet, and phone bills to save on recurring expenses.

8. Increase Your Income Streams

- **Explore Additional Income Opportunities:** Consider freelance work, part-time jobs, or monetizing hobbies to increase your income.

- **Leverage Existing Skills:** Offer services like tutoring, consulting, or writing to generate extra income.

- **Invest in Upskilling:** Consider taking up courses or certifications that can lead to higher-paying job opportunities or promotions.

9. Monitor Your Progress Regularly

- **Set Milestones:** Break your savings goal into smaller, achievable milestones (e.g., quarterly or annual goals) to track your progress.

- **Review and Adjust Your Plan:** Regularly review your savings plan and make adjustments based on changes in income, expenses, or financial goals.

- **Stay Disciplined and Motivated:** Celebrate small wins and milestones to stay motivated. Avoid dipping into your down payment savings for non-emergencies.

10. Leverage Financial Products for Savings

- **Use Tax-Saving Instruments:** Utilize tax-saving options such as Equity-Linked Savings Schemes (ELSS), PPF, or National Savings Certificates (NSC) to maximize your tax benefits while saving.

- **Consider Real Estate Savings Plans:** Some banks and financial institutions offer savings plans specifically designed for down payments, combining savings with returns.

11. Stay Prepared for Unexpected Expenses

- **Build an Emergency Fund:** Maintain an emergency fund of 6-12 months' expenses to handle unexpected costs without dipping into your down payment savings.
- **Insure Yourself Adequately:** Ensure you have adequate health, life, and other insurance coverage to protect against unforeseen expenses.

12. Consider Family Assistance and Gifts

- **Seek Family Support:** If feasible, consider financial assistance or a loan from family members to help meet the down payment requirement.
- **Utilize Gifts and Windfalls:** Use any financial gifts, bonuses, or windfalls (e.g., inheritance, tax refunds) to boost your down payment fund.

Summary of Your Down Payment and Savings Strategy

1. Determine Down Payment Amount and Timeline
2. Evaluate Current Financial Situation
3. Create a Dedicated Savings Account
4. Automate Savings
5. Explore Investment Options
6. Cut Down Non-Essential Expenses
7. Increase Income Streams
8. Monitor Progress and Adjust Plan
9. Leverage Financial Products for Savings
10. Prepare for Unexpected Expenses
11. Consider Family Assistance and Gifts

Sample Plan to Save for a Down Payment

- Property Price: ₹50 lakhs
- Down Payment Required (20%): ₹10 lakhs
- Savings Timeline: 3 years (36 months)
- Monthly Savings Required: ₹27,778

UNDERSTANDING YOUR CREDIT SCORE AND HOW TO IMPROVE IT

Understanding and improving your credit score is crucial for securing a home loan and getting favourable terms in India. Here's a detailed guide on what you need to know about your credit score and how to enhance it:

1. What is a Credit Score?

- Definition: A credit score is a numerical representation of your creditworthiness, based on your credit history and financial behaviour.

- Range: In India, credit scores typically range from 300 to 900. A score above 750 is generally considered excellent and increases your chances of securing a home loan at favourable rates.

2. Components of a Credit Score

- Payment History (35%): Reflects your track record of paying credit accounts on time. Late payments, defaults, and settlements negatively impact your score.

- Credit Utilization (30%): Indicates the ratio of your current credit card balances to your credit limits. High utilization rates can lower your score.

- Credit History Length (15%): The duration for which you've had credit accounts. A longer credit history generally positively affects your score.

- Types of Credit (10%): The mix of credit accounts (e.g., credit cards, instalments loans) you have. A diverse mix can be beneficial.

- New Credit Inquiries (10%): The number of recent inquiries into your credit report. Frequent applications for new credit can reduce your score.

3. Checking Your Credit Score

- Obtain Your Credit Report: You can get your credit report for free from credit bureaus like CIBIL, Equifax, Experian, and CRIF High Mark in India. You are entitled to one free credit report per year from each bureau.

- Review for Accuracy: Check your credit report for errors, outdated information, or fraudulent activities. Dispute any inaccuracies with the credit bureau to have them corrected.

4. Understanding Credit Report Components

- Credit Accounts: List of all your credit accounts, including credit cards, loans, and their current status (active, closed, etc.).

- Payment History: Details of your payment behaviour, including missed or delayed payments.

- Credit Utilization: Current balances on your credit accounts compared to your credit limits.

- Credit Inquiries: Record of recent inquiries into your credit report.

- Public Records: Information on bankruptcies, legal judgments, or other public records affecting your credit.

5. Tips to Improve Your Credit Score

- **Pay Your Bills on Time:**
  - Make Timely Payments: Ensure all bills, including credit cards, loans, and utility bills, are paid on or before the due date.
  - Set Up Reminders: Use reminders or automatic payments to avoid missing due dates.

- **Manage Credit Utilization:**
  - Keep Balances Low: Aim to use less than 30% of your available credit limit on credit cards. Lower utilization rates are better for your score.
  - Pay Off Balances: Regularly pay off your credit card balances in full to avoid high utilization.

- **Maintain a Healthy Credit Mix:**
  - Diversify Credit Types: Maintain a mix of credit accounts, such as credit cards, personal loans, and instalments loans, to show you can handle different types of credit responsibly.
  - Avoid Unnecessary Accounts: Do not open multiple new credit accounts in a short period, as this can negatively impact your score.

- **Check Your Credit Report Regularly:**
  - Monitor for Errors: Regularly review your credit report for inaccuracies or fraudulent activity. Dispute any errors with the credit bureau promptly.
  - Track Your Progress: Use credit monitoring tools or services to keep track of your credit score and report changes over time.

- **Avoid High Credit Inquiries:**
  - Limit New Applications: Apply for new credit only when necessary. Multiple hard inquiries in a short period can reduce your credit score.
  - Understand Inquiry Types: Differentiate between hard inquiries (which impact your score) and soft inquiries (which do not affect your score).

- **Improve Your Credit History Length:**
  - Keep Old Accounts Open: Avoid closing old credit accounts, as they contribute to the length of your credit history and positively impact your score.
  - Maintain Accounts in Good Standing: Ensure all active accounts are managed responsibly and remain in good standing.

- **Resolve Outstanding Debts:**
  - Clear Delinquent Accounts: Pay off any overdue or delinquent accounts and work to resolve collections or defaults.
  - Negotiate Settlements: If you have difficulty paying, negotiate settlements or payment plans with creditors.

6. Benefits of a Good Credit Score

- Better Loan Terms: Higher credit scores often lead to lower interest rates, higher loan amounts, and better terms on home loans and other credit products.

- Easier Loan Approval: A good credit score increases your chances of loan approval and reduces the likelihood of rejection.

- Higher Credit Limits: Lenders may offer higher credit limits on credit cards and loans if you have a strong credit score.

- Lower Insurance Premiums: Some insurance companies offer lower premiums to individuals with good credit scores.

7. Long-Term Credit Management

- Build and Maintain Good Credit Habits: Continuously practice good credit management habits to maintain or improve your credit score over time.

- Plan for Major Purchases: Use your good credit score to your advantage when making significant financial decisions, such as buying a home or car.

8. Tools and Resources

- Credit Monitoring Services: Consider using credit monitoring services to keep track of your credit score and receive alerts on changes.

- Financial Advisors: Consult financial advisors or credit counsellors for personalized advice on improving your credit score and managing your finances.

Summary

1. Understand Your Credit Score Components
2. Check Your Credit Report Regularly
3. Pay Your Bills on Time
4. Manage Credit Utilization
5. Maintain a Healthy Credit Mix
6. Avoid High Credit Inquiries
7. Resolve Outstanding Debts
8. Benefits of a Good Credit Score
9. Long-Term Credit Management

Improving your credit score takes time and consistent effort. By following these guidelines and maintaining good credit practices, you can enhance your creditworthiness and increase your chances of securing a favourable home loan in India.

CHAPTER 3

PRE-APPROVAL AND FINANCING OPTIONS

Getting a pre-approval and understanding your financing options are essential steps in the home-buying process in India. Pre-approval helps you determine how much you can borrow, strengthens your negotiating position, and streamlines the loan process once you've found a property. Here is a comprehensive guide to obtaining pre-approval and exploring financing options available to homebuyers in India.

1. What is Pre-approval for a Home Loan?

- **Definition:** Pre-approval is a preliminary assessment by a lender to determine how much they are willing to lend to you based on your financial situation. It involves evaluating your income, credit score, debts, and other factors.

- **Validity:** Typically valid for 3 to 6 months, giving you time to search for a property with the assurance of financing.

2. Benefits of Getting Pre-approval

- **Know Your Budget:** Understand the maximum loan amount you can obtain, helping you set a realistic budget for your home search.

- **Improves Negotiating Power:** Pre-approval shows sellers that you are a serious buyer with financing ready, which can strengthen your negotiation position.

- **Streamlines the Loan Process:** Speeds up the loan approval process once you have identified a property, as much of the paperwork is already completed.

- **Identifies Potential Issues Early:** Highlights any potential issues with your creditworthiness that you can address before finalizing a property.

3. Steps to Get Pre-approved for a Home Loan in India

Step 1: Gather Your Documents

Prepare the necessary documents to apply for pre-approval:

- **Proof of Identity:** Aadhar card, PAN card, passport, voter ID, or driving license.

- **Proof of Address:** Utility bills, rent agreements, or bank statements.

- **Income Proof:** Salary slips (last 3-6 months), Form 16, income tax returns (ITR) for the last 2-3 years, or audited financial statements for self-employed individuals.

- **Bank Statements:** Statements from all bank accounts for the last 6-12 months.

- **Employment Proof:** Employment letter or certificate.

- **Existing Loan Details:** Details of any existing loans or credit card debt.

- **Property Documents (if applicable):** If you have already identified a property, the sale deed, property tax receipts, and other relevant documents.

Step 2: Choose a Lender

- **Research Lenders:** Compare lenders based on interest rates, loan terms, processing fees, and customer service. Look for banks or housing finance companies (HFCs) with favourable terms.

- **Consider Pre-Approval Offers:** Some lenders provide specific pre-approval offers, such as reduced interest rates or minimal processing fees.

Step 3: Submit the Pre-approval Application

- **Apply Online or In-Person:** Most banks and HFCs in India offer online applications for pre-approval, or you can visit a branch to apply in person.

- **Provide Necessary Information:** Fill out the application form with your personal, employment, and financial details, and submit the required documents.

Step 4: Undergo Credit Evaluation

- **Credit Check:** The lender will assess your credit score, income stability, and debt-to-income ratio. A higher credit score and stable income improve your chances of pre-approval.

- **Financial Assessment:** The lender will calculate your eligibility based on your monthly income, existing debts, and the Loan-to-Value (LTV) ratio.

Step 5: Receive Pre-approval Decision

- **Pre-approval Letter:** If approved, you will receive a pre-approval letter stating the loan amount, interest rate, loan tenure, and other terms and conditions.

- **Review the Terms:** Carefully review the terms, including the loan amount, interest rate, and any conditions that may apply.

4. Financing Options for Homebuyers in India

Option 1: Home Loans from Banks

- **Public Sector Banks:** State Bank of India (SBI), Punjab National Bank (PNB), Bank of Baroda, etc.
  - **Pros:** Lower interest rates, longer tenure, lower processing fees, and government-backed stability.
  - **Cons:** Stricter eligibility criteria, longer processing times, and more documentation.

- **Private Sector Banks:** HDFC Bank, ICICI Bank, Axis Bank, Kotak Mahindra Bank, etc.
  - **Pros:** Faster processing, more flexible terms, and attractive offers for specific customer segments.
  - **Cons:** Slightly higher interest rates compared to public sector banks.

Option 2: Housing Finance Companies (HFCs)

- **Examples:** HDFC Ltd., LIC Housing Finance, Indiabulls Housing Finance, Bajaj FinServ, etc.
  - **Pros:** Specialized focus on home loans, more flexible eligibility criteria, and higher LTV ratios.
  - **Cons:** Higher interest rates and additional charges.

Option 3: Pradhan Mantri Awas Yojana (PMAY)

- **Overview:** A government scheme providing interest subsidies on home loans for first-time homebuyers in the Economically Weaker Section (EWS), Low Income Group (LIG), and Middle-Income Group (MIG).
  - **Subsidy Rates:** Interest subsidy of up to 6.5% for loans up to ₹6 lakh for EWS and LIG, and 3-4% for loans up to ₹12-18 lakh for MIG.
  - **Eligibility:** Must not own a house at the time of application and meet specific income criteria.

Option 4: Loans Against Provident Fund (PF)

- **Eligibility:** Employees can withdraw from their PF for the down payment or construction of a house, provided they have completed at least 5 years of service.
  - **Pros:** Interest-free withdrawal, no need to repay the amount.
  - **Cons:** Reduces retirement savings and may affect future financial security.

Option 5: Employer Home Loan Schemes

- **Overview:** Some employers offer home loan schemes or subsidies for their employees.
  - **Pros:** Lower interest rates and flexible repayment options.
  - **Cons:** Limited availability and may come with employment-based restrictions.

Option 6: Personal Loans for Down Payment

- **Overview:** If you lack sufficient savings for a down payment, you can consider a personal loan.
  - **Pros:** Quick disbursement and no collateral required.
  - **Cons:** Higher interest rates (compared to home loans) and shorter repayment periods.

5. Key Factors to Consider When Choosing a Financing Option

- **Interest Rates:** Compare fixed and floating interest rates. Fixed rates provide stability, while floating rates may offer savings if market rates decline.

- **Loan Tenure:** Choose a tenure that balances EMI affordability with total interest cost. Longer tenures reduce EMIs but increase total interest paid.

- **Loan-to-Value (LTV) Ratio:** Understand the maximum LTV ratio offered by the lender, which affects your down payment requirement.

- **Processing Fees and Charges:** Factor in processing fees, administrative charges, and prepayment or foreclosure penalties.

- **Prepayment and Foreclosure Options:** Look for lenders that offer flexibility in prepaying or foreclosing the loan without heavy penalties.

- **Customer Service and Support:** Consider the lender's customer service quality, responsiveness, and digital banking capabilities.

6. How to Choose the Right Financing Option

- **Compare Multiple Lenders:** Use online tools, financial advisors, or visit various banks and HFCs to compare offers.

- **Assess Your Risk Appetite:** Decide between fixed and floating interest rates based on your financial stability and risk appetite.

- **Align with Long-Term Goals:** Choose an option that aligns with your long-term financial goals, such as minimizing interest costs or ensuring lower monthly EMIs.

- **Consider Tax Benefits:** Evaluate the tax benefits available under Sections 80C and 24(b) of the Income Tax Act for principal and interest repayment, respectively.

7. Finalizing the Loan

- **Lock-in Interest Rate:** Once pre-approved, you may lock in your interest rate to protect against rate hikes.

- **Complete the Application Process:** Provide any additional documentation required and complete the formal loan application once you finalize the property.

- **Loan Disbursement:** Upon approval, the loan amount will be disbursed directly to the seller or builder.

Summary of Steps to Get Pre-approval and Choose Financing Options in India

1. **Get Pre-approved for a Home Loan**
   - Gather documents, choose a lender, submit the application, undergo a credit check, and receive the pre-approval letter.

2. **Explore Financing Options**
   - Evaluate banks, HFCs, government schemes, PF loans, employer schemes, and personal loans.

3. **Compare and Choose the Best Option**
   - Consider factors such as interest rates, tenure, LTV ratio, fees, and customer service.

4. **Finalize and Disburse the Loan**
   - Lock in the interest rate, complete the loan application, and proceed with the disbursement.

By understanding your pre-approval process and financing options, you can make informed decisions and smoothly navigate the path to homeownership in India.

DIFFERENT TYPES OF LOANS

In India, there are various types of loans available for homebuyers, each catering to different needs, eligibility criteria, and financial situations. While terms like "FHA" and "VA" are specific to the U.S., there are analogous options in India that serve similar purposes. Here's an overview of the different types of home loans available in India:

1. Conventional Home Loans

- **Definition:** Traditional loans offered by banks and housing finance companies (HFCs) that are not backed by the government.
- **Features:**
  - Available for the purchase of new or resale homes, construction of a new house, or renovation.
  - Fixed or floating interest rates.
  - Requires a down payment, usually 10-20% of the property value.
  - Loan tenure typically ranges from 5 to 30 years.
- **Eligibility Criteria:**
  - Good credit score (750+), stable income, and debt-to-income ratio within permissible limits.
  - Age and employment stability are also considered.
- **Pros:**
  - Flexibility in loan tenure.
  - Wide choice of lenders.
  - Potentially lower interest rates for eligible applicants.
- **Cons:**
  - Higher down payment requirement.
  - Stricter eligibility criteria compared to government-backed options.

2. Home Loans under the Pradhan Mantri Awas Yojana (PMAY)

- **Definition:** Government-backed loans under the PMAY scheme aimed at providing affordable housing to all eligible sections by 2022.

- **Features:**
  - Offers interest subsidies for Economically Weaker Section (EWS), Low Income Group (LIG), and Middle-Income Group (MIG) segments.
  - Subsidy on interest rates of up to 6.5% for loans up to ₹6 lakh (EWS/LIG) and 3-4% for loans up to ₹12-18 lakh (MIG).
  - Tenure up to 20 years.
- **Eligibility Criteria:**
  - First-time homebuyers who do not own a "pucca" house.
  - Adherence to income criteria: Up to ₹3 lakh (EWS), ₹3-6 lakh (LIG), ₹6-12 lakh (MIG-I), ₹12-18 lakh (MIG-II).
- **Pros:**
  - Lower EMIs due to subsidized interest rates.
  - Encourages homeownership among low and middle-income groups.
- **Cons:**
  - Limited to specific income groups.
  - Requires adherence to PMAY's guidelines and documentation.

3. Home Loans from Banks

- **Public Sector Banks:**
  - **Examples:** State Bank of India (SBI), Punjab National Bank (PNB), Bank of Baroda.
  - Generally, offer lower interest rates, especially for women and senior citizens.
  - Longer loan tenure up to 30 years.
  - **Pros:** Lower interest rates, especially for government employees, and strong branch network.
  - **Cons:** Stricter documentation and longer processing times.
- **Private Sector Banks:**
  - **Examples:** HDFC Bank, ICICI Bank, Axis Bank, Kotak Mahindra Bank.

- Slightly higher interest rates but faster processing and less stringent documentation requirements.
- **Pros:** Quicker processing, more customer-friendly services, and online loan management options.
- **Cons:** Higher interest rates and additional charges.

4. Housing Finance Companies (HFCs) Loans

- **Definition:** Loans provided by specialized institutions like HDFC Ltd., LIC Housing Finance, Indiabulls Housing Finance, etc.
- **Features:**
  - Higher Loan-to-Value (LTV) ratios, which means a lower down payment requirement.
  - Often more flexible in eligibility criteria compared to banks.
- **Eligibility Criteria:**
  - More lenient in terms of credit score and documentation.
- **Pros:**
  - Flexible eligibility and repayment terms.
  - Higher LTV ratios.
- **Cons:**
  - Slightly higher interest rates compared to banks.
  - Additional administrative fees.

5. Loans Against Property (LAP)

- **Definition:** Secured loans where the borrower pledges an existing property as collateral to raise funds.
- **Features:**
  - Can be used for any purpose, including purchasing a home, business expansion, medical expenses, etc.
  - Lower interest rates than personal loans due to collateral security.
  - Loan amount depends on the property value, generally up to 50-60% of its market value.

- **Eligibility Criteria:**
  - ♦ Requires ownership of a residential or commercial property.
- **Pros:**
  - ♦ Lower interest rates compared to unsecured loans.
  - ♦ Longer tenure and larger loan amounts.
- **Cons:**
  - ♦ Risk of property foreclosure in case of default.
  - ♦ Longer processing times due to property valuation.

6. Bridge Loans

- **Definition:** Short-term loans for homebuyers who wish to purchase a new property before selling their existing one.
- **Features:**
  - ♦ Helps bridge the gap between the purchase of a new home and the sale of the old one.
  - ♦ Typically offered for a tenure of up to 2 years.
- **Eligibility Criteria:**
  - ♦ Requires ownership of an existing property and intent to purchase another.
- **Pros:**
  - ♦ Short-term solution for buyers in transition.
- **Cons:**
  - ♦ Higher interest rates due to short-term nature.
  - ♦ Risk of paying two EMIs if the old property does not sell quickly.

7. NRI Home Loans

- **Definition:** Home loans tailored for Non-Resident Indians (NRIs) who wish to buy property in India.
- **Features:**
  - ♦ Similar terms and conditions as domestic home loans but with additional documentation requirements.
  - ♦ Eligibility depends on the NRI's income, age, and employment stability abroad.

- **Pros:**
  - Facilitates property purchase for NRIs.
  - Competitive interest rates.
- **Cons:**
  - More stringent documentation, including proof of NRI status, overseas income, and employment.

8. Home Construction Loans

- **Definition:** Loans specifically designed for individuals who wish to construct a house on a plot of land they already own.
- **Features:**
  - Disbursed in stages based on the construction progress.
  - Covers costs related to raw materials, labour, and other construction expenses.
- **Eligibility Criteria:**
  - Proof of land ownership and construction plan approval by local authorities.
- **Pros:**
  - Tailored for self-construction, with flexibility in disbursement.
  - Can be customized based on construction stages.
- **Cons:**
  - Requires detailed project plan and approvals, which may delay the loan process.

9. Composite Loans

- **Definition:** Loans that combine a plot loan and a home construction loan, allowing borrowers to purchase land and finance the construction of a house simultaneously.
- **Features:**
  - Disbursed in stages, with the initial amount for land purchase and subsequent amounts for construction phases.
  - Lower interest rates compared to separate loans.

- ■ **Pros:**
  - ◆ Convenient for buyers who want to buy land and build a house.
  - ◆ Lower total cost compared to separate loans.
- ■ **Cons:**
  - ◆ Requires detailed documentation and project approvals.

10. Top-Up Home Loans

- ■ **Definition:** Additional loans provided on an existing home loan for various purposes, such as home improvement, renovation, or personal needs.
- ■ **Features:**
  - ◆ Offered to existing home loan borrowers who have a good repayment track record.
  - ◆ Lower interest rates than personal loans.
- ■ **Eligibility Criteria:**
  - ◆ Existing home loan account with a satisfactory repayment history.
- ■ **Pros:**
  - ◆ Lower interest rates compared to personal loans.
  - ◆ No additional collateral required.
- ■ **Cons:**
  - ◆ Limited to the amount already repaid on the existing home loan.

Summary

India offers a range of home loan options to suit different needs:

- ■ **Conventional Home Loans** from banks and HFCs for general home purchases.
- ■ **PMAY Loans** for affordable housing with interest subsidies.
- ■ **Specialized Loans** such as LAP, NRI loans, and home construction loans for specific needs.
- ■ **Bridge Loans, Composite Loans, and Top-Up Loans** for unique financing situations.

Choosing the right loan depends on your financial situation, eligibility, and specific home-buying needs.

FIXED vs VARIABLE RATES: WHICH IS RIGHT FOR YOU?

Choosing between a fixed or variable (floating) interest rate for a home loan in India depends on various factors, including your financial situation, risk appetite, and market conditions. Let's explore the differences between the two types, their pros and cons, and help you decide which option might be right for you.

1. Fixed Interest Rate

A **fixed interest rate** remains constant throughout the loan tenure or for a specified period (usually the first 2-10 years of the loan). The interest rate is locked in at the time of loan approval and does not fluctuate with market changes.

Pros of Fixed Interest Rate:

- **Predictability:** Your monthly EMIs (Equated Monthly Instalments) remain the same throughout the fixed period, making it easier to budget and manage your finances.

- **Protection from Rate Hikes:** You are shielded from any increase in interest rates due to market fluctuations, economic changes, or policy rate adjustments by the Reserve Bank of India (RBI).

- **Stability:** Offers financial stability and peace of mind for those who prefer not to deal with the uncertainty of changing rates.

Cons of Fixed Interest Rate:

- **Higher Initial Rates:** Fixed rates are generally 1-2% higher than the prevailing floating rates to compensate lenders for the risk of future interest rate hikes.

- **Limited Benefits if Rates Fall:** If market rates decline, you won't benefit from the reduced rates, and your EMIs will remain higher than those with floating rates.

- **Prepayment Penalties:** Many lenders charge a prepayment penalty or foreclosure charge on fixed-rate loans if you pay off the loan early or switch to a floating rate.

Who Should Opt for Fixed Rates?

- **First-Time Buyers:** Those who prefer stability and certainty in their monthly payments, especially if they are new to homeownership.

- **Risk-Averse Borrowers:** Individuals with a low risk tolerance who want to avoid market volatility.

- **Stable Economic Conditions:** When interest rates are expected to rise, or are already low, locking in a fixed rate can be advantageous.

2. Floating (Variable) Interest Rate

A **floating interest rate** changes over time based on market conditions, typically linked to a benchmark rate such as the RBI's repo rate, Marginal Cost of Funds-Based Lending Rate (MCLR), or an external benchmark (e.g., T-bill rates). Your loan's interest rate can increase or decrease depending on these benchmarks.

Pros of Floating Interest Rate:

- **Lower Initial Rates:** Floating rates are usually lower than fixed rates, resulting in lower initial EMIs.

- **Benefit from Rate Cuts:** When market rates decrease, your EMIs also decrease, allowing you to save on interest costs.

- **No Prepayment Penalties:** Most lenders do not charge prepayment or foreclosure penalties on floating rate loans, giving you the flexibility to pay off the loan early or switch lenders.

Cons of Floating Interest Rate:

- **Unpredictable EMIs:** Your EMIs can fluctuate, making it harder to plan and budget over the long term.

- **Risk of Rate Hikes:** If interest rates increase due to market conditions or RBI policy changes, your EMIs will rise, leading to higher overall interest costs.

- **Emotional and Financial Stress:** Variable rates can create anxiety, especially if you are unable to handle sudden increases in EMIs.

Who Should Opt for Floating Rates?

- **Market-Savvy Borrowers:** Those who can monitor market trends and make informed decisions based on economic conditions.

- **Flexible Budgets:** Individuals who have a flexible budget and can accommodate potential increases in monthly payments.

- **Shorter Loan Tenure:** Borrowers planning to repay the loan quickly (in less than 5-10 years) may benefit more from floating rates, as they might capitalize on lower rates in the short term.

3. Factors to Consider When Choosing Between Fixed and Floating Rates in India

1. Market Conditions and Rate Trends:

- **Rising Rates:** If you expect interest rates to rise in the near future, a fixed rate might be preferable to lock in lower rates and protect yourself from increases.

- **Falling Rates:** If rates are expected to fall or remain stable, a floating rate could allow you to benefit from lower EMIs and reduced interest costs.

2. Loan Tenure:

- **Shorter Tenure (Up to 10 Years):** Floating rates may be more suitable if you plan to repay the loan quickly, as the interest rate fluctuation impact is lesser over a shorter period.

- **Longer Tenure (More than 10 Years):** A fixed rate can offer more stability and peace of mind for those who prefer predictable payments over a longer period.

3. Personal Financial Situation:

- **Stable Income:** Borrowers with stable income sources (e.g., salaried employees) may prefer fixed rates to ensure consistent EMIs.

- **Irregular Income:** Self-employed individuals or those with variable income might prefer floating rates, especially if they can make prepayments when they have surplus funds.

4. Risk Appetite:

- **Low Risk Tolerance:** If you are uncomfortable with the idea of your EMIs fluctuating due to market conditions, a fixed rate will provide more certainty.

- **High Risk Tolerance:** If you are comfortable with some uncertainty and willing to take advantage of potential rate cuts, a floating rate could be the better option.

5. Economic Outlook:

- **Inflation and RBI Policy Changes:** Monitor inflation rates, RBI monetary policy updates, and the global economic outlook to anticipate future interest rate trends. This will help you make an informed decision on whether to choose a fixed or floating rate.

4. Hybrid or Semi-Fixed Rate Loans: A Middle Ground

Many lenders in India also offer **hybrid or semi-fixed rate loans,** which combine the benefits of both fixed and floating rates.

Features of Hybrid Loans:

- **Fixed Rate for an Initial Period:** The interest rate is fixed for a specified period (usually 2-5 years).

- **Floating Rate Thereafter:** After the fixed-rate period ends, the loan switches to a floating rate based on prevailing market conditions.

- **Flexibility and Stability:** Provides initial stability with the potential to benefit from lower rates in the future.

Who Should Opt for Hybrid Loans?

- **Undecided Borrowers:** Those who are unsure about market trends or their financial situation and want both short-term stability and long-term flexibility.

- **Moderate Risk Tolerance:** Borrowers comfortable with an initial fixed rate but open to the possibility of fluctuating rates later.

5. Summary: Fixed vs. Floating Interest Rates in India

Aspect	Fixed Rate	Floating Rate
EMI Stability	Remains constant throughout the fixed period	Fluctuates based on market conditions
Initial Rate	Typically, higher	Typically, lower
Market Risk	No exposure to rate hikes	Exposed to both rate hikes and rate cuts
Prepayment Charges	Often has penalties	Usually, no penalties
Suitability	Low risk appetite, stable income, rising rate environment	High risk appetite, flexible budget, falling/stable rate environment
Best for	Long-term borrowers, risk-averse individuals	Short-term borrowers, market-savvy individuals

Summary: Which is Right for You?

- Choose a **Fixed Rate** if you value stability and predictability in your EMIs, are a first-time homebuyer, or expect interest rates to rise.

- Opt for a **Floating Rate** if you are willing to take some risk, want to benefit from potential rate cuts, and can manage fluctuating payments.

- Consider a **Hybrid Loan** if you want to start with stability but are open to future changes.

Ultimately, the choice depends on your financial goals, comfort with risk, and understanding of the current and projected economic environment

MORTGAGE LENDERS VS BROKERS: CHOOSING BEST FIT

When choosing between mortgage lenders and brokers in India, it's important to understand the roles each plays in the home-buying process and how they can help you secure the best possible loan. Here is a detailed breakdown of what mortgage lenders and brokers do, the pros and cons of working with each, and how to determine which might be the best fit for you.

1. Mortgage Lenders

Mortgage lenders are financial institutions that provide home loans directly to borrowers. These include banks, non-banking financial companies (NBFCs), and housing finance companies (HFCs). When you approach a lender, you deal directly with them for everything from loan application to disbursement.

Types of Mortgage Lenders in India:

- **Public Sector Banks:** State Bank of India (SBI), Punjab National Bank (PNB), Bank of Baroda, etc.

- **Private Sector Banks:** HDFC Bank, ICICI Bank, Axis Bank, Kotak Mahindra Bank, etc.

- **Housing Finance Companies (HFCs):** HDFC Ltd., LIC Housing Finance, DHFL, Indiabulls Housing Finance, etc.

- **Non-Banking Financial Companies (NBFCs):** Bajaj Finserv, Tata Capital, Aditya Birla Finance, etc.

Pros of Working with a Mortgage Lender:

- **Direct Control:** You deal directly with the lending institution, which can streamline communication and reduce the chance of misunderstandings.

- **Lower Fees:** Lenders often have lower fees because there is no intermediary (broker) involved. This can reduce the overall cost of the loan.

- **Established Reputation:** Many large banks and HFCs have established reputations, providing a sense of security and reliability.

- **Special Offers and Discounts:** Banks often have special schemes, interest rate discounts, and concessions for specific customer segments (e.g., women, government employees).

Cons of Working with a Mortgage Lender:

- **Limited Options:** You are limited to the products offered by that particular lender. If their terms or interest rates aren't competitive, you won't have access to better deals elsewhere.

- **Rigid Criteria:** Banks and financial institutions often have strict eligibility criteria, making it harder for applicants with low credit scores or irregular income to qualify.

- **Less Personalized Service:** Lenders may not always offer the same level of personalized service as brokers, who work specifically on your behalf to find the best deal.

Who Should Choose a Mortgage Lender?

- **Borrowers with Strong Credit Profiles:** Those with good credit scores, stable income, and straightforward loan requirements may find it easier and more cost-effective to work directly with a lender.

- **Those Seeking Lower Fees:** Borrowers looking to avoid intermediary fees and prefer dealing directly with their lender.

- **First-Time Homebuyers Seeking Guidance:** Some lenders, particularly larger banks, offer educational resources and customer support that can be helpful for first-time buyers.

2. Mortgage Brokers

Mortgage brokers act as intermediaries between borrowers and multiple lenders. They work on behalf of the borrower to find and compare different home loan products across various lenders to secure the best rates and terms.

Pros of Working with a Mortgage Broker:

- **Access to Multiple Lenders:** Brokers have relationships with a wide range of lenders, allowing them to offer you multiple loan options from different banks, NBFCs, and HFCs.

- **Personalized Service:** Brokers typically provide a more personalized service, understanding your specific needs and helping you find the best fit.

- **Better Rates for Complex Cases:** Brokers are skilled in negotiating better rates or terms for clients with complex profiles, such as self-employed individuals or those with lower credit scores.

- **Time-Saving:** Brokers handle most of the paperwork, coordination, and communication with lenders, saving you time and effort.

Cons of Working with a Mortgage Broker:

- **Broker Fees:** Brokers charge a commission or fee for their services, which can add to the overall cost of obtaining a mortgage. This fee may be paid by you, the borrower, or the lender.

- **Potential Conflicts of Interest:** Some brokers may be incentivized to direct borrowers to specific lenders that pay higher commissions, which may not always align with the best interest of the borrower.

- **Limited Availability of Lenders:** Not all lenders work with brokers. Therefore, you may miss out on deals from certain banks or financial institutions.

Who Should Choose a Mortgage Broker?

- **Borrowers with Complex Financial Profiles:** Individuals with unique circumstances (e.g., self-employed, low credit scores) who may benefit from the broker's expertise in finding suitable loan options.

- **Time-Conscious Borrowers:** Those who prefer to delegate the legwork of researching and comparing loan products to an experienced professional.

- **First-Time Homebuyers Needing Guidance:** Buyers who need extra guidance and support through the process and want access to multiple loan options.

3. Key Differences Between Mortgage Lenders and Brokers in India

Table of Mortgage Lenders vs Mortgage Brokers/ DSA

Aspect	Mortgage Lenders	Mortgage Brokers or Direct Selling Agents (DSA)
Direct Lending	Yes, provides loans directly to borrowers	No, acts as an intermediary between borrower and lenders
Loan Options	Limited to the lender's own products	Access to multiple loan products from different lenders
Fees	Typically lower, no broker fees	Broker fees may apply (either from borrower or lender)
Personalized Service	Less personalized, more standardized	High level of personalized service and guidance
Flexibility	May have rigid eligibility criteria	More flexible, can find options for different profiles
Processing Time	Direct but can vary depending on the lender	Can be faster since brokers handle most of the paperwork and coordination
Interest Rates	Can offer competitive rates, but limited options	May negotiate better rates due to access to multiple lenders
Best for	Simple, straightforward loans, borrowers with good credit	Complex cases, borrowers looking for multiple options

4. Factors to Consider When Choosing Between a Lender and a Broker

1. Your Financial Profile:

- **Strong Credit Score:** If you have a strong credit score and a stable income, you may get good deals directly from a lender.
- **Low Credit Score or Irregular Income:** If you have a low credit score, are self-employed, or have irregular income, a broker might be able to find you a lender willing to work with you.

2. Time and Effort:

- **Willingness to Shop Around:** If you have the time and are comfortable comparing loan products from different lenders, going directly to a lender could save you money.

- **Need for Convenience:** If you prefer a one-stop-shop and want to save time, a broker can provide a more streamlined experience.

3. Loan Complexity:

- **Simple Loan Needs:** If you need a straightforward loan with standard terms, going directly to a lender might be sufficient.

- **Complex Loan Requirements:** If you require special terms, need a loan product tailored to unique circumstances, or are looking for the lowest possible interest rate, a broker can provide valuable assistance.

4. Cost Sensitivity:

- **Concern About Fees:** If you are concerned about additional costs, going directly to a lender may avoid broker fees.

- **Willing to Pay for Expertise:** If you value expert advice and are willing to pay for it, a broker can help you navigate the complexities of the mortgage market.

5. Summary: Mortgage Lender vs. Broker - Which is the Best Fit for You?

- **Choose a Mortgage Lender if:**
  - You have a straightforward loan requirement and a good credit profile.
  - You prefer dealing directly with the financial institution to avoid additional broker fees.
  - You are confident in your ability to compare loan options and negotiate terms.

- **Choose a Mortgage Broker if:**
  - You have a complex financial profile or need a loan tailored to unique circumstances.
  - You want access to a variety of loan products from multiple lenders and need personalized advice.

- ♦ You are looking for convenience and time-saving, with a broker handling much of the legwork.

Ultimately, the decision comes down to your specific needs, financial situation, and comfort level with navigating the loan process.

PART 2

FINDING YOUR DREAM HOME

CHAPTER 4

DEFINING YOUR HOME CRITERIA

Identifying Your Needs vs Wants

When buying a home, especially as a first-time homebuyer in India, it's crucial to distinguish between your needs and wants. This helps you focus on essential aspects of the property that are non-negotiable, while also recognizing desirable features that can be compromised if necessary. Clarifying your needs versus wants can save you time, reduce stress, and help you make a more informed decision that aligns with your budget and lifestyle.

1. Understanding Needs vs. Wants in Home Buying

- **Needs:** These are the non-negotiable aspects of a home that are essential for your daily living and overall well-being. Needs usually relate to factors like safety, functionality, and basic living requirements.

- **Wants:** These are the desirable features that would enhance your comfort, convenience, or lifestyle but are not essential. Wants often reflect personal preferences and lifestyle choices and can be sacrificed if they do not fit within your budget.

2. Common Needs and Wants for Homebuyers in India

Here's a breakdown of some common needs and wants when purchasing a home in India:

Needs (Essentials)

1. Location Proximity:

- Close to work, schools, hospitals, and public transport.
- Access to essential services like markets, banks, and medical facilities.

2. Budget Compatibility:

- The home price and associated costs (maintenance, taxes, etc.) should fit comfortably within your budget.

3. Size and Space Requirements:

- Sufficient number of bedrooms and bathrooms for the family size.
- Adequate living and storage space to meet your immediate and future needs.

4. Safety and Security:

- Secure neighbourhood with low crime rates.
- Gated communities or buildings with security guards, CCTV, and other security measures.

5. Basic Amenities:

- Access to essential amenities like water supply, electricity, sanitation, and waste management.

6. Legal Compliance:

- Clear property titles, up-to-date taxes, necessary approvals, and permissions from local authorities.
- Compliance with RERA (Real Estate Regulatory Authority) norms and regulations.

7. Future Growth Potential:

- A location with good growth prospects, appreciation potential, or infrastructure development plans.

Wants (Desirables)

1. Aesthetic Preferences:

- Modern architecture, stylish interiors, and specific design elements.

2. Additional Amenities:

- Gym, swimming pool, clubhouse, or children's play area within the community.

3. **Higher Floor or View:**

  ♦ Preferences for higher floors, sea views, garden views, or cityscape views.

4. **Luxury Features:**

  ♦ Modular kitchen, premium fittings, smart home technology, or designer finishes.

5. **Extra Space:**

  ♦ Additional rooms like a home office, guest room, or servant quarters.

6. **Outdoor Spaces:**

  ♦ Balconies, terraces, or private gardens.

7. **Parking Facilities:**

  ♦ Reserved or covered parking, additional parking space for visitors.

3. Steps to Identify Your Needs vs. Wants

Step 1: Evaluate Your Lifestyle and Future Plans

- Current Lifestyle: Assess your daily routines, commute times, work-from-home needs, family size, and any specific lifestyle preferences.

- Future Considerations: Consider any plans to expand your family, accommodate elderly parents, or shift jobs, which may affect your space, location, and budget requirements.

Step 2: Determine Your Budget and Financial Limits

- Loan Eligibility: Assess your loan eligibility, monthly EMIs you can comfortably afford, and the down payment required.

- Hidden Costs: Consider additional costs like registration fees, maintenance charges, property taxes, and home insurance.

Step 3: Prioritize Based on Necessity and Feasibility

- Make a list of features and categorize them into "needs" and "wants."

- Rank these based on their importance, urgency, and impact on your daily life.

- For example, if you work from home frequently, a quiet home office space might be a "need," while a swimming pool could be a "want."

Step 4: Research the Market and Analyse Options

- **Property Visits:** Visit multiple properties to understand what features are standard in your budget and location.

- **Compare Options:** Compare similar properties to identify which ones meet most of your needs and some of your wants within your budget.

Step 5: Reevaluate and Adjust Your List as Needed

- Be flexible and willing to adjust your expectations as you explore the market.

- Reevaluate your list if you find that your "wants" significantly exceed your budget or if certain "needs" are too difficult to fulfil.

4. Practical Tips for Balancing Needs vs. Wants

1. Create a Detailed Checklist:

- Make a checklist of all features you consider essential (needs) and desirable (wants). Use this checklist during property visits to evaluate each option objectively.

2. Consider Resale Value and Investment Potential:

- Focus on properties with good resale value, even if they lack some of your "wants." Key factors affecting resale value include location, legal clearances, and basic amenities.

3. Don't Compromise on Non-Negotiables:

- Stick to your core needs, such as location, safety, budget, and legal compliance. Avoid compromising on these, as they impact your long-term comfort and financial health.

4. Be Ready to Compromise on Some "Wants":

- Be flexible on the "wants" that do not significantly affect your quality of life. For example, you may forgo a higher floor for a more affordable or conveniently located property.

5. Seek Professional Advice:

- ♦ Consult with real estate professionals, brokers, or property advisors to gain insights into market trends, neighbourhood growth prospects, and potential trade-offs.

6. Factor in Future Changes:

- ♦ Think about potential lifestyle changes, such as a growing family or a job change, and how these could impact your needs. Choose a home that can accommodate these future changes.

5. Examples of Needs vs. Wants in Home Buying

Category	Needs	Wants
Location	Close to workplace, schools, or medical facilities	Proximity to shopping malls, entertainment, or recreational areas
Budget	Fits within your approved loan amount and down payment ability	Room for renovation or upgrade costs
Space	Minimum of 2-3 bedrooms and 2 bathrooms	Extra guest room, home office, or larger living area
Amenities	24/7 water supply, electricity backup, and waste management	Gym, swimming pool, club membership
Safety	Secure neighbourhood, CCTV surveillance, or gated community	Smart home security features
Legal Compliance	Clean title, approved building plans, and RERA registration	N/A
Interior Features	Basic kitchen and bathroom fittings	Modular kitchen, premium tiles, and high-end fixtures

6. Summary: Striking the Right Balance

By clearly identifying your needs versus wants, you can make a more focused and confident decision about your home purchase in India. This process helps you prioritize essentials while still considering additional features that enhance your living experience. Remember, buying a home is a long-term commitment, so focus on what matters most to your quality of life, both now and in the future.

LOCATION, NEIGHBOURHOOD AND MARKET RESEARCH

When buying a home in India, selecting the right **location** and understanding the **neighbourhood** are crucial steps that can significantly affect your quality of life, future resale value, and return on investment. Thorough **market research** helps you make an informed decision, ensuring you buy a property in a location that suits your lifestyle and meets your financial and investment goals.

1. Importance of Location in Home Buying

The location of your home is arguably the most important factor in determining not only the property's value but also its appreciation potential over time. It influences several aspects:

- **Convenience and Accessibility:** Proximity to work, schools, healthcare facilities, shopping areas, and public transportation.

- **Lifestyle and Comfort:** Availability of social and recreational facilities, such as parks, gyms, restaurants, and entertainment options.

- **Safety and Security:** Crime rates, neighbourhood security, and access to emergency services.

- **Growth Potential:** Infrastructure development, such as new roads, metro lines, business hubs, and government initiatives in the area.

- **Resale Value:** Properties in prime locations or emerging neighbourhoods tend to appreciate more over time, offering better resale value.

2. Key Factors to Consider When Choosing a Location in India

A. Proximity and Connectivity

- **Work and Daily Commute:** Choose a location that minimizes your daily commute time and costs. Proximity to employment hubs or business districts is essential.

- **Schools and Colleges:** If you have children, proximity to good schools, colleges, and educational institutions should be a priority.

- **Healthcare Facilities:** Easy access to hospitals, clinics, and pharmacies is important for emergencies and regular health check-ups.

- **Public Transport:** Access to public transport like metro stations, bus stops, and railway stations can add convenience and reduce commuting costs.

- **Road Connectivity:** Check the road network quality and connectivity to major highways, airports, and other important locations.

B. Safety and Security

- **Crime Rates:** Research crime statistics in the area. Check with local police stations or community reports.

- **Gated Communities and Security Measures:** Look for areas with gated communities, CCTV surveillance, and neighbourhood watch programs.

C. Neighbourhood Amenities

- **Daily Essentials:** Proximity to supermarkets, grocery stores, banks, ATMs, and petrol stations.

- **Recreational Facilities:** Parks, gyms, community centres, sports facilities, and entertainment options like malls and multiplexes.

- **Dining and Social Life:** Nearby cafes, restaurants, and cultural or social hubs can enhance your lifestyle.

D. Future Growth Potential

- **Infrastructure Development:** Consider areas where there are ongoing or planned infrastructure projects (e.g., metro expansion, new highways, or smart city initiatives). These can increase property values over time.

- **Government Policies:** Locations with government-backed development projects, special economic zones (SEZs), or urban renewal schemes often experience higher growth.

- **Employment Opportunities:** Look for areas near upcoming business districts, IT parks, and industrial corridors.

E. Environmental Factors

- **Air Quality:** Consider the pollution levels in the area, especially in large cities.

- **Noise Levels:** Avoid locations near busy roads, railway lines, or industrial areas if noise is a concern.
- **Green Spaces:** Proximity to parks, lakes, and green belts can provide a healthier living environment and better quality of life.

F. Local Community and Culture

- **Demographics:** Understand the demographic composition of the neighbourhood to ensure it aligns with your lifestyle and preferences.
- **Community Engagement:** Some areas have a strong sense of community, which can be a positive aspect for families or individuals looking to build social connections.

3. Conducting Neighbourhood Research in India

A. Online Research and Tools

- **Property Portals:** Use online property portals like Magic Bricks, 99acres, Housing.com, and Common Floor to explore properties in different neighbourhoods. These platforms provide information on price trends, nearby amenities, and user reviews.
- **Google Maps:** Use Google Maps to explore the locality, check distances to important places, and get a feel of the neighbourhood using Street View.
- **Social media and Forums:** Join local community groups on platforms like Facebook, Reddit, or local forums to understand the experiences of current residents.
- **Crime Reports:** Some websites and apps provide crime statistics for specific areas, or you can contact local police stations for insights.

B. Site Visits

- **Daytime and Night time Visits:** Visit the area during different times of the day and week to gauge traffic, noise levels, and overall safety.
- **Walk Around the Neighbourhood:** Walk around to observe the local amenities, street cleanliness, road quality, and general upkeep.

- **Speak to Locals:** Talk to people living in the area to gather firsthand information about the neighbourhood's pros and cons.

C. Consult Real Estate Experts

- **Local Agents:** Work with local real estate agents who have a deep understanding of the neighbourhood. They can provide insights into price trends, upcoming projects, and potential risks.

- **Property Lawyers:** Consult with property lawyers to ensure the property has a clear title and there are no legal disputes or zoning issues.

- **Valuers and Inspectors:** Hire professional valuers and property inspectors to assess the property's condition and ensure its value aligns with the market rate.

4. Market Research for Property Buying in India

A. Understanding Market Trends

- **Property Price Trends:** Track historical price trends in the area to understand appreciation potential. Look for consistent growth over the years.

- **Rental Yield:** Check the rental yield if you are buying as an investment. Areas with high demand for rentals typically provide better returns.

- **Inventory Overhang:** Research if there is an inventory overhang (unsold units) in the area. A high inventory overhang can indicate oversupply, potentially impacting property values negatively.

- **Absorption Rate:** This is the rate at which homes are sold in a specific market. High absorption rates can suggest strong demand and potential for price appreciation.

B. Analyzing Demand and Supply

- **Local Demand Drivers:** Identify what drives demand in the area — such as proximity to an IT park, upcoming metro line, or good schools.

- **Supply Dynamics:** Evaluate the number of new projects coming up. Excessive new supply can stabilize or lower property prices in the short term.

- **Market Cycles:** Be aware of the real estate market cycle (recovery, expansion, hyper-supply, and recession) to determine the best time to buy.

C. Evaluating Property Appreciation Potential

- **Past Performance:** Look at how the property prices in the area have performed in the past 5 to 10 years.

- **Planned Developments:** Research any planned infrastructure developments, such as new roads, metro lines, airports, or commercial hubs, which can drive future appreciation.

- **Zoning Regulations:** Check local zoning regulations and development plans. Changes in zoning (e.g., converting agricultural land to residential use) can affect property values.

5. Practical Tips for Effective Market Research in India

1. **Use Multiple Sources:** Rely on multiple sources, such as online portals, local agents, government websites, and direct site visits, to get a comprehensive view.

2. **Stay Updated on Local News:** Follow local news sources and real estate blogs to stay informed about new developments, infrastructure projects, or policy changes affecting the area.

3. **Attend Property Expos:** Property expos are a great way to meet multiple developers, understand different offerings, and get a sense of market sentiment.

4. **Network with Real Estate Professionals:** Engage with real estate agents, property consultants, and local market experts who have insights into upcoming trends and opportunities.

5. **Analyze Developer Reputation:** Research the track record of developers in the area to avoid projects with delays, poor construction quality, or legal disputes.

6. Summary: Making an Informed Decision

Location, neighbourhood, and market research are foundational elements of buying a home in India. A well-chosen location with good connectivity, safety, and growth potential not only enhances your quality of life but also provides significant financial benefits over time. By conducting thorough market research, you can identify the best areas to invest in and make a decision that aligns with your lifestyle, budget, and future goals.

UNDERSTANDING DIFFERENT TYPES OF PROPERTIES: SINGLE FAMILY, CONDO, TOWNHOUSE ETC.

When buying a home in India, understanding the different types of properties available is essential to finding the right fit for your lifestyle, budget, and long-term plans. Each property type comes with its unique features, advantages, and limitations. Here's a comprehensive overview of the common types of properties available in India:

1. Single-Family Homes

Definition:

A **single-family home** is an independent, standalone residential structure designed for one family. It typically has its own plot of land, boundaries, and is not attached to any other residential unit.

Features:

- Full ownership of the house and the land it stands on.
- Offers maximum privacy as there are no shared walls with neighbours.
- Typically larger in size, with multiple bedrooms, bathrooms, and private outdoor spaces like a garden or backyard.
- Common in suburban and semi-urban areas.

Pros:

- Greater control over the property, allowing for customizations and renovations.
- More space and privacy.
- Usually comes with private amenities like gardens, parking, and sometimes even a pool.

Cons:

- Higher maintenance costs and responsibilities for upkeep.
- Generally, more expensive to buy compared to apartments or townhouses.
- Limited security features unless located in a gated community.

Ideal for:

Families looking for privacy, space, and the freedom to modify their home.

2. Condominiums (Condos)

Definition:

A **condominium** (or condo) is a type of residential property where you own an individual unit within a larger building or complex, and share ownership of common areas like hallways, gardens, swimming pools, and parking spaces.

Features:

- Typically, high-rise buildings with multiple units.
- Common areas are maintained by a homeowners' association (HOA) or a resident welfare association (RWA).
- Amenities like security, gym, pool, clubhouse, and community spaces are often included.

Pros:

- Lower maintenance responsibilities since the HOA/RWA handles common area upkeep.
- Access to shared amenities such as gyms, pools, and parks.
- Generally, more affordable than single-family homes or villas.

Cons:

- Less privacy due to shared walls and common areas.
- Monthly maintenance fees and potential restrictions on renovations or pets.
- Limited control over property management decisions.

Ideal for:

Young professionals, small families, and retirees looking for a low-maintenance lifestyle with access to community amenities.

3. Townhouses

Definition:

A **townhouse** is a multi-story residential property that shares one or more walls with adjacent units but has its own entrance and sometimes a small private garden or backyard.

Features:

- Typically, 2-3 stories high, with separate floors for living, dining, and bedrooms.
- Combines the benefits of a single-family home and an apartment; more space and privacy than a condo but less than a standalone home.
- Usually, part of a larger community or complex with shared amenities.

Pros:

- More space and privacy compared to a condo, with fewer maintenance responsibilities than a single-family home.
- Access to shared community amenities like parks, gyms, and playgrounds.
- Generally, more affordable than single-family homes.

Cons:

- Less privacy than a standalone home due to shared walls.
- May have HOA/RWA fees for maintenance of common areas.
- Limited ability to make exterior changes or renovations.

Ideal for:

Families or individuals who want more space and privacy than a condo offers but are not ready for the responsibilities of a single-family home.

4. Villas

Definition:

A **villa** is a luxury residential property, typically a standalone structure, located within a gated community or a premium neighborhood. Villas offer a high level of privacy, space, and exclusivity.

Features:

- Usually larger in size, with multiple bedrooms, bathrooms, private gardens, and sometimes a private pool.
- Often part of a gated community with high-end amenities like clubhouses, gyms, tennis courts, and security.
- Can be single-story or multi-story and designed with a focus on aesthetics, luxury, and privacy.

Pros:

- High level of privacy and exclusivity.
- Access to luxury amenities within the community.
- Greater freedom to customize and modify the property.

Cons:

- Expensive to buy and maintain.
- Higher property taxes and utility costs.
- May not be located in central or urban areas, often found in suburban or semi-urban locations.

Ideal for:

High-net-worth individuals, large families, and those seeking a luxury living experience with privacy and exclusivity.

5. Apartments (Flats)

Definition:

An **apartment** (or flat) is a self-contained residential unit that is part of a larger building, often a high-rise, with shared facilities and common areas.

Features:

- Available in various configurations (1BHK, 2BHK, 3BHK, etc.) depending on the number of bedrooms, hall, and kitchen.
- Amenities like elevators, security, parking, and maintenance services are often included.
- Typically located in urban or semi-urban areas, close to workplaces and public transport.

Pros:

- Affordability, especially in major cities where land is scarce.
- Low maintenance, as upkeep of common areas is handled by the building management or RWA.
- Access to shared amenities like pools, gyms, and playgrounds.

Cons:

- Less privacy and control over noise levels.
- Limited freedom to make structural changes or major renovations.
- Monthly maintenance charges for common areas and amenities.

Ideal for:

Individuals, young professionals, small families, or retirees looking for a convenient, low-maintenance living arrangement in urban areas.

6. Penthouses

Definition:

A **penthouse** is a luxurious apartment located on the top floor of a high-rise building, often featuring expansive layouts, private terraces, and exclusive amenities.

Features:

- Larger floor area, often with multiple bedrooms, private outdoor spaces, and panoramic views.
- Premium interiors, high ceilings, and exclusive amenities such as private elevators or pools.
- Often located in prime locations within the city.

Pros:

- Ultimate privacy within an apartment building.
- Luxurious living space with premium features and amenities.
- High resale value due to exclusivity and demand.

Cons:

- Very expensive to purchase and maintain.
- Limited to urban locations, often in high-density areas.
- Higher maintenance fees due to larger space and luxury amenities.

Ideal for:

Affluent buyers seeking a high-end lifestyle with the convenience of urban living.

7. Studio Apartments

Definition:

A **studio apartment** is a small, self-contained unit that typically combines the living, dining, and sleeping areas into a single space, with a separate bathroom.

Features:

- Compact design, ideal for single occupants or couples.
- Often located in urban areas close to work hubs and public transport.
- Lower maintenance and utility costs due to the smaller size.

Pros:

- Affordable option for singles or young professionals.
- Low utility and maintenance costs.
- Easy to maintain and clean.

Cons:

- Limited space and privacy.
- Not suitable for families or those requiring separate rooms.
- Limited scope for customization.

Ideal for:

Single professionals, students, or couples looking for a budget-friendly, low-maintenance living option in the city.

8. Co-operative Housing Societies

Definition:

A **co-operative housing society** is a residential society where the residents collectively own the property and manage it through a cooperative society.

Features:

- The property is owned collectively, and residents own shares in the society rather than individual apartments.
- Decisions regarding maintenance, renovations, and rules are made collectively by the society members.
- Common in major cities like Mumbai, where land is scarce.

Pros:

- Strong sense of community and collective decision-making.
- Generally lower costs compared to independent ownership.
- Access to shared amenities.

Cons:

- Less privacy and autonomy over property decisions.
- Decisions require consensus, which can be time-consuming.
- Restrictions on renting or selling properties due to society rules.

Ideal for:

Those looking for a strong community environment, particularly in cities like Mumbai where co-operative societies are common.

9. Builder Floors

Definition:

A **builder floor** is a residential unit in a low-rise building, usually constructed by a private builder on a single plot. Each floor is an independent unit with its entrance.

Features:

- More privacy than apartments, as there are fewer units per building.
- Offers the feeling of living in an independent home at a lower cost.
- Customizable interiors, with fewer restrictions from developers or societies.

Pros:

- Greater privacy and fewer shared facilities.
- Customization options for interiors.
- Usually has dedicated parking space and fewer maintenance charges.

Cons:

- Limited amenities compared to high-rise apartments.
- Maintenance responsibility falls on the owner.
- Potential legal issues with land titles if not properly vetted.

Ideal for:

Families seeking privacy and customization options without the cost of a standalone home.

Summary: Choosing the Right Property Type in India

Selecting the right property type depends on your lifestyle, budget, location preferences, and future plans. Each type of property offers different advantages and trade-offs, so consider what aspects matter most to you—be it privacy, space, amenities, or cost. Whether you prefer the convenience of a condo, the luxury of a villa, or the privacy of a single-family home, understanding these options will help you make an informed decision.

FUTURE RESALE POTENTIAL: THINKING LONG-TERM

When buying a home in India, considering the future resale potential is a key factor that can influence your decision, especially if you view your home as both a place to live and an investment. Resale potential depends on several factors, including location, property type, market conditions, and future developments in the area. Thinking long-term involves evaluating these factors to ensure your property appreciates in value over time, providing good returns if you decide to sell.

1. Key Factors Influencing Resale Potential in India

A. Location and Neighborhood

- **Proximity to Key Areas:** Properties closer to employment hubs, commercial centres, schools, hospitals, and public transport generally have higher demand and better resale value.

- **Quality of Infrastructure:** Good Road connectivity, public transportation, and access to utilities like water, electricity, and waste management are essential. Proximity to metro lines, highways, and airports can also significantly boost resale potential.

- **Safety and Security:** Low crime rates and well-maintained public spaces are attractive to potential buyers. Gated communities and areas with active neighborhood associations are often preferred.

- **Emerging Areas:** Investing in emerging neighbourhoods or areas with planned infrastructure development (such as new metro lines, flyovers, or commercial zones) can lead to higher appreciation over time.

B. Type of Property

- **Property Type Popularity:** Some types of properties, like apartments and townhouses, tend to have higher demand due to their affordability and convenience. Single-family homes or villas might have a niche market but could appreciate significantly in premium or well-developed areas.

- **Size and Configuration:** Properties with 2-3 bedrooms (2BHK or 3BHK) are generally more popular due to the demand from nuclear families. Smaller units like 1BHKs might have limited appeal, while larger properties (4BHK and above) cater to a niche segment.

- **Amenities and Facilities:** Properties in complexes with amenities like swimming pools, gyms, playgrounds, and community halls are more attractive to buyers, especially families. Modern facilities such as elevators, power backup, and security systems add value.

- **Property Age and Condition:** Newer properties generally have higher resale value. However, well-maintained older properties can also be appealing, especially if they are in prime locations.

C. Developer Reputation

- **Brand Value:** Properties built by reputed developers tend to command a premium price due to perceived higher construction quality, better amenities, and greater trust in legal compliance.

- **Track Record of Timely Delivery:** Developers known for completing projects on time and adhering to promises regarding quality and amenities attract more buyers and investors.

- **Resale Market Activity:** Projects by well-known developers often have active resale markets, making it easier to sell your property.

D. Market Conditions and Trends

- **Real Estate Cycles:** Understanding the property market cycle (recovery, expansion, hyper-supply, or recession) can help determine the best time to buy or sell. Buying during a downturn and selling during an upswing can maximize returns.

- **Supply and Demand Dynamics**: Areas with high demand and limited supply tend to see better appreciation rates. Conversely, regions with an oversupply of properties might experience slower price growth or stagnation.

- **Government Policies:** Policies related to real estate, such as the Real Estate Regulatory Authority (RERA), Goods and Services Tax (GST), and affordable housing incentives, can impact property prices and resale value.

E. Future Development and Infrastructure Projects

- **Infrastructure Upgrades:** Upcoming infrastructure projects like new metro lines, flyovers, airports, or business parks can significantly boost property values in the surrounding areas.

- **Zoning Changes:** Changes in zoning regulations, such as converting land use from agricultural to residential or commercial, can increase property demand and prices.

- **Urban Development Plans:** Government-backed urban renewal projects or smart city initiatives can lead to rapid appreciation in property values in the targeted areas.

F. Legal and Documentation Clarity

- **Clear Title and Documentation:** Properties with clear titles, proper registration, and no pending legal issues are easier to sell and attract more buyers.

- **Compliance with Regulations:** Properties that comply with local building codes, environmental regulations, and other statutory requirements have better resale prospects.

- **Encumbrance Status:** Ensure the property is free from any mortgages or liens, as encumbrances can deter buyers and lower resale value.

2. Evaluating Long-Term Appreciation Potential

A. Conducting Market Research

- **Price Trends Analysis:** Track historical price trends in the area to understand how property values have appreciated over time. Consistent growth indicates strong market demand.

- **Rental Yield Analysis:** High rental yields can suggest a robust market and future resale potential, especially in cities with strong rental demand.

- **Absorption Rate:** A high absorption rate (ratio of sold properties to available properties) indicates a healthy market with good demand, which can positively impact resale potential.

B. Studying Future Developments

- **Local Government Plans:** Check municipal or regional development plans for information on upcoming infrastructure projects, zoning changes, or new commercial/industrial developments.

- **Private Sector Developments:** Be aware of new commercial or residential projects, such as shopping malls, business hubs, and IT parks, as they can increase demand for nearby housing.

- **Urbanization Trends:** Rapid urbanization in cities and towns often leads to increased demand for housing, improving resale prospects.

C. Understanding Buyer Preferences

- **Demographic Trends:** Consider buyer demographics, such as young professionals, families, or retirees, and their preferences for property types, sizes, and locations.

- **Lifestyle Changes:** Changes in lifestyle preferences, such as the growing demand for eco-friendly homes, smart homes, or properties in gated communities, can impact resale values.

- **Accessibility Needs:** Properties that offer better accessibility for seniors or are close to public transport can appeal to a wider range of buyers, enhancing resale prospects.

3. Steps to Maximize Resale Value

A. Maintenance and Upkeep

- **Regular Maintenance:** Regularly maintain the property to keep it in good condition. Address issues like plumbing, electrical, and structural problems promptly to prevent them from affecting property value.

- **Renovations and Upgrades:** Invest in necessary upgrades, such as modernizing kitchens and bathrooms, repainting, or enhancing energy efficiency with better windows and insulation.

- **Curb Appeal:** Maintain a well-kept exterior with attractive landscaping, fresh paint, and clean surroundings to create a positive first impression for potential buyers.

B. Documentation and Compliance

- **Ensure Clear Documentation:** Keep all property documents, including sale deeds, encumbrance certificates, property tax receipts, and building approvals, up to date and in order.

- **Adhere to Local Regulations:** Ensure the property complies with local building codes, fire safety regulations, and environmental guidelines.

C. Leverage Market Timing

- **Sell at the Right Time:** Monitor the market for optimal selling conditions, such as low inventory levels, high demand, or favourable economic indicators.

- **Consider Holding During Downturns:** If market conditions are unfavourable (such as during a recession or market correction), consider holding the property until conditions improve.

D. Engage Real Estate Professionals

- **Hire a Reputable Real Estate Agent:** Experienced agents can provide insights into local market conditions, help set a competitive price, and market the property effectively.

- **Use Professional Services:** Utilize property valuers, lawyers, and home inspectors to assess the property's condition, value, and legal status to attract serious buyers.

4. Best Locations for Resale Potential in India

- **Tier-1 Cities:** Major metros like Mumbai, Delhi, Bengaluru, Hyderabad, Chennai, Pune, and Kolkata generally have higher demand and better resale value due to job opportunities, infrastructure development, and urban growth.

- **Emerging Tier-2 Cities:** Cities like Ahmedabad, Jaipur, Coimbatore, Lucknow, Indore, and Visakhapatnam are becoming popular due to rapid urbanization, growing IT sectors, and government initiatives, offering good appreciation potential.

- **Upcoming Suburbs:** Suburban areas with good connectivity to city centers and proximity to infrastructure projects, such as Navi Mumbai, Noida, Gurgaon, Whitefield (Bengaluru), and Gachibowli (Hyderabad), are witnessing rapid growth and appreciation.

Summary: Thinking Long-Term for Resale Potential

To maximize the future resale potential of your property in India, focus on choosing the right location, understanding the market dynamics, and staying informed about future developments. Keep your property well-maintained, comply with legal regulations, and consider buyer preferences to ensure your investment appreciates over time. With careful planning and market insight, you can position your property for strong returns in the future.

CHAPTER 5

THE HOME SEARCH PROCESS

How to Effectively Search For Homes

Effectively searching for homes in India requires a strategic approach, combining online tools, offline resources, and local market knowledge to find the right property that fits your needs and budget. Here's a step-by-step guide on how to efficiently search for homes in India:

1. Define Your Requirements

Before you start your search, it's important to have a clear understanding of your needs and preferences. Consider the following factors:

- **Budget:** Determine your budget, including the maximum amount you are willing to spend on the property. Factor in additional costs such as registration fees, stamp duty, property taxes, maintenance charges, and brokerage fees.

- **Location:** Decide on preferred locations or neighborhoods based on factors like proximity to your workplace, schools, hospitals, shopping centers, public transport, and lifestyle preferences. Consider both primary and emerging areas that fit your budget.

- **Property Type:** Identify the type of property you want (e.g., apartment, villa, townhouse, builder floor, etc.) based on your family size, lifestyle, and long-term plans.

- **Size and Configuration:** Determine the size of the property (e.g., 1BHK, 2BHK, 3BHK, etc.) and the minimum number of bedrooms and bathrooms needed.

- **Amenities:** List essential and desirable amenities (e.g., parking, security, elevators, power backup, clubhouse, gym, swimming pool, etc.) to refine your search.

- **Future Needs:** Consider future needs, such as the possibility of a growing family, resale value, or rental income potential.

2. Start with Online Property Portals

Online property portals are a great starting point for your home search in India. They provide access to a wide range of property listings, detailed information, and filters to refine your search. Popular online property portals in India include:

- **99acres:** Offers comprehensive listings of residential and commercial properties across India. It includes detailed information on property features, location, price, and developer reputation.

- **Magicbricks:** Provides property listings, including resale, new properties, and rentals. The platform offers neighborhood insights, price trends, and a home loan calculator.

- **Housing.com:** Known for its clean interface and detailed listings, Housing.com provides high-quality photographs, 3D tours, and neighborhood details.

- **NoBroker:** Focuses on direct transactions between buyers and sellers, eliminating brokerage fees. It offers verified property listings and useful neighborhood insights.

- **CommonFloor:** Offers property listings, community forums, and virtual tours, helping buyers make informed decisions.

- **Real Estate Developer Websites:** Visit websites of reputed developers for information on new projects, floor plans, pricing, and special offers.

Tips for Using Online Portals Effectively:

- **Set Filters:** Use filters to narrow down your search based on location, price, property type, size, and amenities.

- **Save Searches:** Save your search criteria and create alerts to receive notifications about new listings that match your preferences.

- **Read Reviews:** Check user reviews and ratings for specific projects, developers, and localities.

- **Use Virtual Tours:** Take advantage of virtual tours and high-quality images to assess properties remotely.

- **Compare Listings:** Compare multiple properties side by side to evaluate price, location, amenities, and other factors.

3. Use Mobile Apps and Social Media

In addition to property portals, mobile apps and social media platforms can be valuable tools in your home search:

- **Mobile Apps:** Download property search apps like 99acres, Magic bricks, and Housing.com to receive instant notifications, access listings on the go, and interact with sellers or agents.

- **Social Media Groups:** Join Facebook groups, WhatsApp groups, and Telegram channels related to real estate in your target city or locality. These groups often have listings from individual sellers, real estate agents, and developers.

- **Instagram and YouTube:** Follow real estate influencers, developers, and agents on Instagram and YouTube for property tours, market insights, and project updates.

4. Leverage Real Estate Agents and Brokers

Real estate agents and brokers can provide valuable assistance in your home search:

- **Local Market Knowledge:** Agents have in-depth knowledge of the local market, including upcoming projects, property prices, and neighborhood trends.

- **Access to Off-Market Listings:** They often have access to off-market listings or properties that are not yet advertised online.

- **Negotiation Skills:** Experienced agents can help negotiate a better deal on your behalf.

- **Legal Assistance:** Agents can guide you through the legal documentation process, ensuring compliance with local regulations and avoiding potential pitfalls.

Tips for Working with Agents:

- **Choose Reputable Agents:** Look for agents with a good reputation, positive reviews, and local expertise. Verify their credentials, such as registration with the Real Estate Regulatory Authority (RERA).

- **Clarify Fees:** Discuss the agent's commission structure and any additional fees upfront to avoid surprises later.

- **Stay Informed:** While agents provide valuable insights, it's important to stay informed and cross-check information from multiple sources.

5. Visit Local Real Estate Exhibitions and Property Fairs

Attending real estate exhibitions and property fairs can provide a firsthand look at multiple properties in a short period:

- **Developer Showcases:** Developers often showcase their new and ongoing projects, providing information on floor plans, pricing, and special offers.

- **Networking Opportunities:** Interact with developers, real estate agents, financial advisors, and other professionals to gain market insights.

- **Discounts and Offers:** Take advantage of special discounts, offers, and pre-launch benefits that are often available at such events.

6. Conduct In-Person Visits and Neighborhood Research

While online tools are valuable, visiting properties in person is crucial for making an informed decision:

- **Schedule Property Visits:** Arrange site visits for shortlisted properties to assess their condition, layout, and surroundings. Verify the quality of construction, space utilization, and amenities.

- **Explore the Neighborhood:** Walk around the neighborhood to evaluate factors like cleanliness, safety, traffic, noise levels, and proximity to essential services (e.g., schools, hospitals, supermarkets).

- **Speak to Residents:** Interact with current residents to get feedback on the property's management, maintenance, and any potential issues.

- **Check Future Developments:** Look for signs of upcoming infrastructure projects, commercial developments, or zoning changes that could impact property values.

7. Verify Legal and Documentation Aspects

Before finalizing a property, thoroughly verify its legal status and documentation:

- **Title Deed Verification:** Ensure the seller has a clear and marketable title to the property, free from any encumbrances or disputes.

- **RERA Registration:** Check if the property is registered under the Real Estate (Regulation and Development) Act (RERA), which mandates transparency and protects buyers' interests.

- **Encumbrance Certificate:** Obtain an encumbrance certificate from the sub-registrar's office to confirm the property is free from mortgages or legal dues.

- **Building Approvals:** Verify that the property has all necessary approvals from local authorities, including building plans, environmental clearances, and occupancy certificates.

- **Check for Litigation:** Conduct a background check to ensure the property is not involved in any legal disputes or litigations.

8. Assess Financing Options and Get Pre-Approved

Understanding your financing options and obtaining pre-approval can streamline your home search:

- **Compare Loan Offers:** Research home loan options from different banks and financial institutions to compare interest rates, loan terms, and processing fees.

- **Check Eligibility:** Verify your eligibility for home loans based on factors like income, credit score, and employment status. Use online loan calculators to estimate monthly EMIs and total loan costs.

- **Get Pre-Approved:** Obtain pre-approval from a bank or financial institution to strengthen your negotiating position with sellers and expedite the buying process.

9. Leverage Government Schemes and Incentives

Explore government schemes and incentives that can help make homeownership more affordable:

- **Pradhan Mantri Awas Yojana (PMAY):** Check your eligibility for the PMAY scheme, which offers interest subsidies to first-time homebuyers from economically weaker sections, low-income groups, and middle-income groups.

- **Stamp Duty Concessions:** Look for state-specific stamp duty concessions and exemptions available for women buyers, first-time buyers, or affordable housing.

10. Evaluate Long-Term Prospects and Resale Potential

Consider the long-term prospects of the property, including:

- **Future Appreciation:** Assess the potential for property value appreciation based on factors like location, infrastructure development, and market trends.

- **Rental Income:** Evaluate the potential for rental income if you plan to lease the property in the future.

- **Resale Value:** Consider factors that could impact resale value, such as the property's age, condition, and popularity of the location.

11. Make an Informed Decision

After thorough research and evaluation, narrow down your options and make an informed decision:

- **Conduct Due Diligence:** Ensure all legal checks and documentation are in order before making an offer.

- **Negotiate the Price:** Use your research and knowledge to negotiate a fair price with the seller.

- **Finalize Financing:** Confirm your home loan approval and finalize the terms with the lender.

- **Close the Deal:** Complete the necessary paperwork, pay the required fees, and register the property in your name.

Summary: A Strategic Approach to Home Search

Effectively searching for homes in India involves a combination of online tools, offline resources, and due diligence. By defining your requirements, leveraging technology, consulting experts, and conducting thorough research, you can find the right home that meets your needs and fits your budget. Staying informed about market trends and legal aspects will help you make a confident and informed decision.

TOURING HOMES AND WHAT TO LOOK FOR

Touring homes is a crucial step in the home-buying process that allows you to evaluate properties in person and get a feel for the space, layout, and overall condition. In India, touring homes involves more than just walking through the property; it's about conducting a thorough assessment of multiple factors, including construction quality, neighborhood dynamics, and potential issues. Here's a comprehensive guide on how to tour homes effectively and what to look for:

1. Preparing for the Home Tour

Before you start visiting properties, take these preparatory steps to make the most of your tours:

- **Schedule Tours Strategically:** Plan your visits to maximize your time. Try to visit multiple properties in the same area on the same day. Schedule tours during daylight hours to better assess natural lighting and any visible defects.

- **Create a Checklist:** Prepare a checklist of your key criteria, such as budget, location, property type, size, amenities, and any specific needs or preferences. This will help you evaluate each property consistently.

- **Bring Necessary Tools:** Carry a notebook, pen, and measuring tape. Consider bringing a camera or smartphone to take photos and videos of the properties for future reference. A flashlight can help inspect dark corners or basements.

- **Dress Comfortably:** Wear comfortable clothing and shoes, especially if you are touring multiple properties in one day. This will help you move around easily and stay focused.

2. What to Look for During a Home Tour in India

When touring homes, it's essential to focus on the following aspects to ensure that the property meets your expectations and is a sound investment:

A. Exterior Inspection

1. Building Structure and Quality

- ♦ **Check for Cracks or Damage:** Look for visible cracks in the walls, ceilings, and foundation. Small hairline cracks may not be a concern, but larger cracks could indicate structural issues.

- **Exterior Finishing:** Examine the condition of the exterior paint, plaster, and any cladding materials. Signs of peeling paint, water stains, or mold growth can indicate water seepage or poor maintenance.

- **Roof Condition:** If you are considering a standalone house or villa, inspect the roof for signs of damage, missing tiles, or water stains. Ensure proper drainage to prevent water accumulation.

- **Building Age and Maintenance:** Note the age of the building and assess its overall maintenance level. Older buildings may require more repairs and maintenance, impacting long-term costs.

2. Surroundings and Neighborhood

- **Street and Access:** Check the condition of the road leading to the property. Look for adequate street lighting, clean surroundings, and ease of access, especially during peak hours or in case of emergencies.

- **Proximity to Amenities:** Assess the proximity to essential services such as schools, hospitals, markets, banks, public transport, and recreational areas. Ensure these amenities meet your lifestyle needs.

- **Noise Levels:** Observe the noise levels around the property. Properties near busy roads, airports, railway lines, or construction sites may experience high noise levels, which can affect comfort.

- **Safety and Security:** Check if the neighborhood appears safe and secure. Look for security measures such as CCTV cameras, gated access, and the presence of security personnel.

3. Parking and Common Areas

- **Parking Availability:** Check if there is adequate parking space for your vehicles. For apartments, ensure that the allotted parking space is easily accessible and well-marked.

  - **Condition of Common Areas:** Evaluate the condition of common areas such as lobbies, corridors, elevators, staircases, and gardens. Poor maintenance of these areas could indicate neglect by the management.

B. Interior Inspection

1. Layout and Space Utilization

- **Functional Layout:** Assess the overall layout and flow of the property. Ensure that the rooms are well-proportioned and that the layout aligns with your lifestyle needs (e.g., open vs. closed kitchens, separate dining areas, etc.).

- **Room Sizes:** Measure room dimensions to ensure they meet your space requirements. Pay attention to the ceiling height, as lower ceilings can make spaces feel cramped.

- **Storage Spaces:** Check for adequate storage options such as closets, cabinets, utility rooms, and built-in shelves. Consider if the available storage meets your needs.

2. Quality of Construction and Finishes

- **Flooring:** Inspect the type and condition of the flooring. Check for loose tiles, uneven surfaces, or signs of damage. Ensure the flooring materials (e.g., vitrified tiles, marble, wooden flooring) are of good quality.

- **Walls and Ceilings:** Look for any visible cracks, water stains, or mold growth on walls and ceilings. These could indicate leakage or dampness issues.

- **Doors and Windows:** Open and close all doors and windows to check for smooth operation. Ensure they are properly aligned, secure, and free from any damage or rot.

- **Kitchen and Bathrooms:** Evaluate the quality of fittings, fixtures, and cabinetry in the kitchen and bathrooms. Check for water pressure, plumbing leaks, drainage, and ventilation. Inspect countertops, tiles, and sanitaryware for damage or wear.

3. Electrical and Plumbing Systems

- **Electrical Outlets and Wiring:** Test electrical outlets, switches, and lighting fixtures to ensure they are functional. Ask about the quality and age of the wiring. Verify the presence of a sufficient number of outlets in each room.

- **Plumbing Fixtures:** Turn on taps and showers to check water pressure and drainage. Look for signs of leaks under sinks, around toilets, and near pipes.

- ◆ **Power Backup:** Verify if the property has a power backup system, such as an inverter or generator, especially in areas prone to frequent power outages.

4. Ventilation and Natural Light

- ◆ **Windows and Airflow:** Check for adequate ventilation in all rooms. Ensure there are enough windows to allow for cross-ventilation and fresh air circulation.
- ◆ **Natural Light:** Observe the amount of natural light entering each room. South-facing properties usually receive more sunlight, while properties facing east or west may have limited natural light.

5. Pest and Infestation Checks

- ◆ **Signs of Infestations:** Look for signs of pest infestations, such as droppings, nests, or holes in woodwork. Pay attention to areas under sinks, behind cabinets, and around windows and doors.

C. Legal and Compliance Aspects

1. Property Documentation

- ◆ **Title Deed:** Ensure the property has a clear and marketable title, free from encumbrances or disputes. Ask for a copy of the title deed to verify ownership.
- ◆ **RERA Registration:** Check if the property is registered with the Real Estate Regulatory Authority (RERA), ensuring transparency and compliance with local regulations.
- ◆ **Approvals and Clearances:** Verify that the property has all necessary approvals, such as building plan approval, environmental clearances, and occupancy certificates from local authorities.

2. Encumbrance Status

- ◆ **Encumbrance Certificate:** Obtain an encumbrance certificate from the sub-registrar's office to confirm the property is free from legal dues, mortgages, or liens.

3. Local Compliance

- ◆ **Check for Deviations:** Ensure there are no unauthorized constructions, deviations from approved plans, or violations of building codes. Unauthorized constructions could lead to legal issues or demolition in the future.

3. Engaging with Sellers and Agents

While touring, engage with the seller or agent to gather more information about the property:

- **Ask About Maintenance History:** Inquire about the property's maintenance history, including recent repairs or renovations, and ask for receipts or records if available.

- **Discuss Neighbours and Community:** Ask about the neighbours and the community culture. This can help you gauge the suitability of the property for your lifestyle.

- **Clarify Utility and Maintenance Costs:** Get an estimate of monthly utility bills (electricity, water, gas) and maintenance costs. Inquire about any pending dues or upcoming charges.

- **Understand the Reason for Sale:** Ask why the current owner is selling the property. This can provide insights into potential issues or opportunities.

4. Evaluating the Property for Future Needs

Think long-term when evaluating a property:

- **Consider Potential for Modifications:** Assess if the property allows for future modifications, such as room extensions, adding a balcony, or upgrading amenities.

- **Check Resale and Rental Potential:** Evaluate the property's potential for appreciation and ease of resale based on location, market trends, and future infrastructure developments.

- **Think About Accessibility:** Consider the accessibility for elderly family members, children, or people with disabilities. Check for features like ramps, elevators, and safety measures.

5. Make Detailed Notes and Comparisons

After each home tour:

- **Take Detailed Notes:** Write down your impressions, pros, and cons of each property while the details are fresh in your mind.

- **Use a Rating System:** Create a rating system (e.g., 1-10) for various criteria such as location, layout, condition, and price to objectively compare properties.

- **Review Photos and Videos:** Revisit photos and videos to recall specific details and evaluate properties side by side.

6. Conduct a Second Visit if Necessary

If you find a property you like, consider scheduling a second visit:

- **Visit at Different Times:** Visit the property at different times of the day (e.g., morning, afternoon, and evening) to assess lighting, noise levels, and neighborhood activity.

- **Bring an Expert:** Bring along a trusted expert, such as a contractor or engineer, to provide a professional opinion on the property's condition.

7. Make an Informed Decision

After thoroughly evaluating all aspects, narrow down your choices:

- **Discuss with Family Members:** Share your observations and seek input from family members or trusted advisors.

- **Negotiate the Price:** If you decide on a property, use your findings to negotiate a fair price with the seller.

- **Consult a Legal Expert:** Engage a legal expert to review all property documents before making an offer.

Summary: Touring Homes with a Critical Eye

Touring homes is an essential part of the home-buying process in India. By carefully inspecting each aspect of the property and its surroundings, asking the right questions, and considering both present needs and future potential, you can make a well-informed decision. A critical eye and thorough due diligence will help ensure that the property you choose is a good fit for you and your family, both now and in the future.

EVALUATING POTENTIAL PROPERTIES: RED FLAGS AND POSITIVE SIGNS

When evaluating potential properties in India, it is crucial to identify both red flags that could indicate future problems and positive signs that suggest a sound investment. This balanced approach will help you make an informed decision that aligns with your needs, budget, and long-term goals.

Red Flags to Watch Out for When Evaluating Properties in India

1. **Legal and Documentation Issues**

   - **Unclear Title Deed:** If the property does not have a clear and marketable title, it may be involved in disputes or have outstanding debts or liens. Always ensure the title deed is free from any encumbrances and is legally transferable.

   - **No RERA Registration:** Properties not registered with the Real Estate Regulatory Authority (RERA) may lack transparency and accountability. Avoid properties that are not RERA-compliant, as they may not meet the necessary regulatory standards.

   - **Lack of Proper Approvals:** Properties without the necessary approvals from local authorities (e.g., building plans, environmental clearances, occupancy certificates) may face legal action or demolition. Verify all required approvals and permits are in place.

   - **Pending Litigation:** Properties involved in legal disputes or court cases can lead to prolonged legal battles, financial loss, or inability to transfer ownership. Conduct a thorough background check for any pending litigation.

2. **Construction Quality Issues**

   - **Visible Cracks or Structural Damage:** Large or numerous cracks in walls, ceilings, or floors may indicate poor construction quality or structural problems. Cracks near beams, columns, or foundations are particularly concerning.

   - **Dampness or Water Seepage:** Signs of dampness, water stains, mold, or peeling paint can indicate water seepage or poor waterproofing. Seepage issues can damage property interiors and affect structural integrity.

♦ **Poor Finishing:** Uneven floors, misaligned doors or windows, and subpar paintwork are signs of shoddy workmanship. These issues may require costly repairs or renovations in the future.

♦ **Temporary Fixtures and Materials:** If the property uses temporary or low-quality materials, such as hollow-core doors, inferior tiles, or substandard fittings, it may indicate cost-cutting measures by the developer or owner.

3. Location and Neighborhood Concerns

♦ **Poor Accessibility:** Properties with inadequate access to major roads, public transport, or essential services may impact your daily convenience and reduce the property's resale value.

♦ **High Noise Levels:** Properties located near busy roads, airports, railway tracks, or industrial areas may suffer from excessive noise pollution, affecting your comfort and quality of life.

♦ **Lack of Basic Amenities:** Evaluate the availability of essential amenities such as schools, hospitals, grocery stores, and parks. A lack of nearby amenities can affect both liveability and future resale value.

♦ **Unfavourable Neighborhood Dynamics:** A high crime rate, poor hygiene, or signs of neglect (e.g., broken streetlights, poor road conditions) in the neighborhood can negatively impact safety, quality of life, and property value.

4. Financial and Market Risks

♦ **Overpriced Property:** Properties priced significantly higher than comparable properties in the area may be difficult to resell or rent out at a profit. Research local market trends and prices to ensure you are getting a fair deal.

♦ **Unfavourable Loan Terms:** Properties with high loan interest rates, low loan-to-value ratios, or restrictive financing options may indicate financial risks. Compare different financing options and choose a reputable lender.

- **Developer's Poor Reputation:** Check the track record of the developer. Delays in project delivery, poor quality construction, or unresolved customer complaints can be red flags. Look for developers with a good reputation, completed projects, and positive customer feedback.

- **Uncertain Market Conditions:** Be cautious if the property is located in an area experiencing market downturns, oversupply, or low demand. This could impact future property appreciation or rental income potential.

5. Property-Specific Red Flags

- **Pest Infestation:** Signs of pest infestation, such as droppings, nests, or chewed materials, can indicate underlying maintenance or hygiene issues.

- **Inadequate Ventilation and Natural Light:** Properties with insufficient windows, poor airflow, or lack of natural light may lead to higher energy bills and uncomfortable living conditions.

- **Frequent Repairs or Maintenance:** If a property requires frequent repairs or has a history of maintenance problems (e.g., plumbing, electrical, or structural issues), it could lead to ongoing costs and inconveniences.

Positive Signs to Look for When Evaluating Properties in India

1. Strong Legal and Documentation Status

- **Clear Title and Ownership:** A property with a clear title and ownership status is a good sign of legal soundness. Verify that all documents are in order, including the sale deed, title deed, encumbrance certificate, and any other relevant approvals.

- **RERA Registration:** Properties registered under RERA are more likely to comply with regulatory standards, provide transparency, and ensure accountability from developers. This reduces the risk of delays and fraudulent practices.

- **Proper Approvals and Certifications:** Properties with all necessary approvals and certifications (e.g., building plans, environmental clearances, occupancy certificates) indicate compliance with local regulations and building codes.

2. Good Construction Quality

- **Well-Maintained Property:** Properties with well-maintained exteriors and interiors, such as clean common areas, fresh paint, and sturdy fixtures, indicate good upkeep and care by the developer or owner.

- **High-Quality Materials:** The use of high-quality construction materials (e.g., solid wood doors, premium tiles, branded sanitaryware) suggests a focus on durability and longevity.

- **Solid Structural Integrity:** Absence of major cracks, dampness, or visible damage to the building's structure is a positive sign. Properties that have withstood natural events (e.g., earthquakes, floods) without damage indicate good construction practices.

- **Reputed Developer or Builder:** Properties built by reputed developers with a proven track record of quality construction, timely delivery, and positive customer feedback are more likely to be reliable investments.

3. Desirable Location and Neighborhood

- **Proximity to Key Amenities:** Properties close to essential services such as schools, hospitals, supermarkets, parks, public transport, and recreational facilities are more convenient and have better resale potential.

- **Good Connectivity:** Properties well-connected to major roads, highways, and public transport networks offer ease of commuting and access to other parts of the city, enhancing their appeal and value.

- **Safe and Clean Environment:** A clean and well-maintained neighborhood with low crime rates, well-lit streets, and good community facilities indicates a safe and comfortable living environment.

- **Upcoming Infrastructure Developments:** Properties located in areas with planned infrastructure projects (e.g., metro lines, highways, commercial hubs) are likely to appreciate in value over time.

4. Favourable Financial and Market Conditions

- **Competitive Pricing:** Properties priced competitively with similar properties in the area offer better investment potential. Conduct a comparative market analysis to ensure you are paying a fair price.

- **Flexible Financing Options:** Availability of multiple financing options, favourable interest rates, and good loan-to-value ratios from reputable banks or financial institutions are positive indicators.

- **Strong Market Demand:** Properties in areas with high demand, low vacancy rates, and rising rental yields indicate a healthy market with potential for appreciation.

- **Government Incentives:** Properties eligible for government schemes and incentives (e.g., Pradhan Mantri Awas Yojana, stamp duty concessions) can provide additional financial benefits.

5. Property-Specific Positive Signs

- **Energy Efficiency and Green Features:** Properties with energy-efficient features (e.g., LED lighting, solar panels, rainwater harvesting, double-glazed windows) can lower utility bills and enhance comfort.

- **Good Ventilation and Natural Light:** Properties with ample windows, cross-ventilation, and natural light contribute to a healthier living environment and reduce reliance on artificial lighting and cooling.

- **Ample Parking and Storage:** Adequate parking space (for apartments or standalone houses) and sufficient storage options (e.g., closets, utility rooms) add to the convenience and appeal of the property.

- **Positive Feedback from Residents:** Feedback from current residents about the property, management, and neighborhood can provide insights into the community's quality and potential challenges.

Summary: Balancing Red Flags and Positive Signs

- When evaluating potential properties in India, a balanced approach is key. Look out for red flags that could indicate future problems or hidden costs, and prioritize properties with positive signs that indicate a sound investment. Conduct thorough due diligence, consult with legal and financial experts, and take your time to assess each property's strengths and weaknesses before making a decision.

PART 3

THE BUYING PROCESS

CHAPTER 6

MAKING THE OFFER AND NEGOTIATION

Understanding the real estate market dynamics and making an appropriate offer are critical steps in the home-buying process in India. Real estate markets can be complex, with various factors influencing property prices, demand, and supply. By analysing these dynamics, you can determine the right offer price that aligns with market conditions and maximizes your investment potential.

UNDERSTANDING MARKET DYNAMICS IN INDIa

To make a well-informed offer, it's essential to understand the market dynamics that influence property prices in India. Here are the key factors to consider:

1. Demand and Supply Dynamics

- **High-Demand Areas:** Locations with strong demand, such as metro cities (e.g., Mumbai, Delhi, Bangalore) or rapidly developing areas with good infrastructure, are likely to have higher property prices and less room for negotiation.

- **Low-Supply Areas:** Areas with limited availability of land, new developments, or properties are likely to see higher property prices due to scarcity.

- **Buyer's Market vs. Seller's Market:**

    - **Buyer's Market:** When supply exceeds demand, buyers have more leverage to negotiate lower prices. This situation is common in areas with high inventory levels or in a slow economy.

♦ **Seller's Market:** When demand exceeds supply, sellers have the upper hand, and property prices tend to be higher. This situation often occurs in high-growth areas or markets with limited available properties.

2. Economic Factors

- **Interest Rates:** Changes in home loan interest rates significantly impact buyer affordability and demand. Lower interest rates typically lead to increased demand, while higher rates may reduce affordability.

- **Inflation and Cost of Living:** Inflation affects construction costs (materials, labour) and property prices. An increase in inflation can lead to higher property prices, whereas stable inflation may keep prices steady.

- **Government Policies:** Policy changes such as tax benefits for first-time homebuyers, interest rate subsidies, changes in stamp duty rates, and affordable housing schemes (like Pradhan Mantri Awas Yojana) can influence demand and market dynamics.

3. Local Market Conditions

- **Location-Specific Factors:** Factors like proximity to workplaces, educational institutions, hospitals, public transport, and commercial hubs can drive demand and affect property prices.

- **Upcoming Infrastructure Projects:** Announcements of new infrastructure projects (e.g., metro extensions, highways, airports) can lead to property price appreciation due to anticipated improvements in connectivity.

- **Neighborhood Trends:** Changes in neighborhood dynamics (such as crime rates, development of commercial centers, or changes in local amenities) can influence property values. A vibrant and growing neighborhood will generally command higher property prices.

4. Property-Specific Factors

- **Property Type and Condition:** The type of property (apartment, villa, commercial, etc.), its age, condition, and unique features (such as amenities, views, and floor plans) significantly affect its market value.

- **Builder Reputation:** Properties developed by reputed builders are generally perceived as more reliable and tend to have higher resale values. On the other hand, lesser-known developers may offer lower prices to attract buyers.

- **Time on Market:** Properties that have been on the market for a long time may indicate overpricing or issues with the property. Sellers of such properties may be more open to negotiation.

5. Seasonal Trends

- **Festive Seasons:** In India, the real estate market often sees increased activity during festive seasons like Diwali and Dussehra, when many people consider it auspicious to buy property. During these times, demand may be higher, and sellers may be less flexible with negotiations.

- **Off-Peak Seasons:** Off-peak seasons (like the monsoon months) may present opportunities for better deals, as fewer buyers are actively looking for properties.

Making an Appropriate Offer: Key Steps

Once you have a clear understanding of the market dynamics, you can make an informed offer. Here's a step-by-step guide to making an appropriate offer in India:

1. Conduct a Comparative Market Analysis (CMA)

- **Research Comparable Properties:** Look for recent sales data of similar properties (in terms of size, type, age, location, and amenities) in the area. This will help you determine the fair market value and understand what other buyers are paying.

- **Analyze Listing Prices vs. Sold Prices:** Compare the asking prices of properties currently on the market with the actual prices of recently sold properties. This can reveal how much negotiation room you may have.

- **Use Online Tools and Platforms:** Use real estate platforms like 99acres, Magic-Bricks, Housing.com, and others to gather data on property prices, trends, and recent transactions in your target area.

2. Evaluate the Property's Condition and Unique Features

- **Inspect the Property:** Conduct a thorough inspection to identify any repairs or renovations needed. Use this information to adjust your offer accordingly.

- **Consider Unique Selling Points:** Evaluate any unique features of the property that add value, such as a corner plot, higher floor with a view, proximity to green spaces, or premium amenities.

3. Understand the Seller's Motivation

- **Gauge the Seller's Urgency:** If the seller is in a hurry to sell (e.g., due to relocation, financial constraints, or a need to close quickly), they may be more open to accepting a lower offer.

- **Identify Seller Preferences:** Some sellers may prefer quick transactions or cash offers over those contingent on financing. Tailoring your offer to meet the seller's preferences can give you an edge in negotiations.

4. Factor in Market Conditions

- **Buyer's Market:** In a buyer's market, consider making an offer below the asking price, as you may have more negotiating power. Aim for a reasonable starting offer (5-10% below asking) and be prepared to negotiate.

- **Seller's Market:** In a seller's market, where competition is high, make a strong initial offer close to the asking price to show serious intent. Consider including favourable terms, such as a flexible closing date, to strengthen your offer.

5. Determine Your Budget and Financial Flexibility

- **Set a Maximum Price:** Determine the maximum amount you are willing to pay for the property, factoring in your budget, loan eligibility, down payment, and future costs (such as maintenance, taxes, and registration fees).

- **Get Pre-Approved for a Loan:** Having a pre-approved loan can enhance your bargaining power, as it shows the seller that you are financially ready and capable of closing the deal quickly.

6. Include a Buffer for Negotiations

- **Start Slightly Lower:** Make an initial offer slightly lower than your maximum budget to allow room for negotiation. Be reasonable and avoid making a lowball offer that could offend the seller or close negotiations.

- **Consider Other Negotiable Aspects:** In addition to the price, consider negotiating on other terms like closing costs, possession timelines, repairs, or inclusion of furniture and fixtures.

7. Draft a Formal Offer

- **Include All Relevant Terms:** A formal offer should outline the purchase price, payment terms, contingencies (such as home inspection or financing approval), possession date, and any additional requests (e.g., repairs or furnishings).

- **Use a Professional Real Estate Agent or Lawyer:** Engaging a real estate agent or lawyer can help you draft a legally sound offer letter that protects your interests and adheres to local regulations.

8. Be Prepared for Counteroffers

- **Expect Negotiations:** Be prepared for the seller to counter your initial offer. Stay flexible, be willing to compromise, and use your research and findings to support your negotiation points.

- **Know When to Walk Away:** If the seller is unwilling to negotiate within your budget or terms, be prepared to walk away. Don't let emotions drive your decision; focus on making a rational, well-informed choice.

Additional Tips for Making an Appropriate Offer in India

- **Leverage Market Trends:** Use data on local market trends to justify your offer price. If prices are declining or stagnating, highlight this to strengthen your position.

- **Be Polite and Professional:** Maintain a respectful and courteous tone during negotiations. Building rapport with the seller or their agent can facilitate smoother negotiations.

- **Highlight Your Buyer Profile:** If you are a first-time buyer, have a pre-approved loan, or are ready to close quickly, emphasize these factors to make your offer more attractive to the seller.

Summary: Aligning Your Offer with Market Realities

Understanding the market dynamics in India and making an appropriate offer involves thorough research, strategic planning, and careful consideration of various factors. By analysing local market conditions, assessing the property's value, and understanding the seller's motivations, you can position yourself to make a fair and competitive offer that meets your financial goals.

KEY TERMS TO INCLUDE IN YOUR OFFER

When making an offer to buy a property in India, it is important to include key terms that clearly outline the conditions of the purchase. These terms help protect both the buyer and the seller by ensuring that all aspects of the transaction are understood and agreed upon. Here are the key terms you should include in your offer:

Key Terms to Include in Your Offer in India

1. Purchase Price

- Definition: The total amount you are willing to pay for the property.
- Details to Include: Specify the exact purchase price in Indian Rupees (INR). Make sure the price aligns with the current market value and your budget.
- Importance: Establishes the basis of the negotiation and reflects the value you assign to the property.

2. Payment Terms

- Definition: The schedule and method of payments you intend to make.
- Details to Include: Include details about the down payment amount, timing (e.g., upon signing the sale agreement), and the balance payment. Mention whether the payments will be made via bank transfer, cheque, or another method.
- Importance: Clarifies how and when payments will be made, reducing potential disputes.

3. Earnest Money Deposit (EMD)

- Definition: A deposit made to show the buyer's serious intent to purchase the property.
- Details to Include: State the amount of the deposit, typically ranging from 1% to 3% of the purchase price. Specify when the deposit will be paid and whether it is refundable in certain circumstances (e.g., if financing is not approved).
- Importance: Demonstrates the buyer's commitment to the transaction and compensates the seller if the buyer backs out without a valid reason.

4. Contingencies

- Definition: Conditions that must be met for the sale to proceed.
- Details to Include:
  - **Financing Contingency:** The offer is contingent on securing a home loan or mortgage approval.
  - **Inspection Contingency:** The offer is contingent on a satisfactory home inspection, where major defects must be repaired or addressed.
  - **Legal Title Verification:** The offer is contingent on a clean and marketable title with no pending legal disputes or encumbrances.
  - **Regulatory Approvals:** The offer is contingent on the necessary government approvals (e.g., RERA registration, building permits).
  - **Importance:** Protects the buyer from unforeseen issues and provides an option to back out or renegotiate the terms.

5. Closing Date

- Definition: The date when the final sale transaction will be completed.
- Details to Include: Specify the proposed closing date (e.g., 30 to 60 days from the acceptance of the offer) when the ownership will be transferred, and the buyer will take possession.
- Importance: Establishes a timeline for completing the transaction and ensures that both parties are aligned on the process.

6. Possession Date

- Definition: The date when the buyer takes physical possession of the property.
- Details to Include: State whether the possession date is the same as the closing date or a different agreed-upon date (e.g., if the seller needs additional time to vacate).
- Importance: Ensures clarity on when the buyer will gain access to the property, avoiding any potential disputes.

7. Fixtures and Inclusions

- **Definition:** Items that are included in the sale of the property.

- **Details to Include:** Clearly list any items that are to be included in the sale, such as appliances, furniture, light fixtures, curtains, and any other fixtures. Specify if certain items will be excluded.

- **Importance:** Prevents misunderstandings about what is and isn't part of the sale, ensuring that both parties have the same expectations.

8. Property Condition and Repairs

- **Definition:** Terms regarding the condition of the property and any repairs that must be made.

- **Details to Include:** Specify that the property will be delivered in the same condition as when inspected. If the inspection reveals any defects, include a list of repairs or concessions requested.

- **Importance:** Protects the buyer from unexpected costs and ensures that the property is in acceptable condition at closing.

9. Transfer Fees and Taxes

- **Definition:** Allocation of responsibility for various taxes and fees related to the property transfer.

- **Details to Include:** Specify who is responsible for paying the stamp duty, registration fees, GST (if applicable), and any other transfer-related charges. Often, the buyer pays the stamp duty and registration fees, while other charges may be negotiable.

- **Importance:** Prevents disputes over payment responsibilities and ensures all legal obligations are met.

10. Title and Legal Clearances

- **Definition:** Assurance that the property has a clear, marketable title.

- **Details to Include:** State that the sale is contingent on the seller providing a clear title and all necessary legal clearances, including a "No Objection Certificate" (NOC) from the relevant authorities, occupancy certificates, and any other required documents.

- ◆ **Importance:** Protects the buyer from potential legal complications or disputes over ownership.

11. Default and Penalty Clauses

- ◆ **Definition:** Terms outlining penalties if either party fails to fulfil their obligations.

- ◆ **Details to Include:** Include details on penalties for delays in payment, failure to meet contingencies, or withdrawal from the agreement without a valid reason.

- ◆ **Importance:** Provides a framework for resolving disputes and compensating the affected party if the other party defaults.

12. Termination Clause

- ◆ **Definition:** Conditions under which the agreement can be terminated by either party.

- ◆ **Details to Include:** Outline circumstances under which the buyer or seller can terminate the agreement (e.g., failure to obtain financing, unsatisfactory inspection, or breach of contract terms).

- ◆ **Importance:** Ensures both parties understand the exit options and reduces the risk of legal disputes.

13. Arbitration and Dispute Resolution

- ◆ **Definition:** The method of resolving disputes if a conflict arises.

- ◆ **Details to Include:** Specify the method of dispute resolution (e.g., arbitration, mediation) and the jurisdiction (city/court) where disputes will be resolved.

- ◆ **Importance:** Provides a clear mechanism for handling disputes, reducing the likelihood of costly and lengthy court battles.

14. Timeframe for Acceptance

- ◆ **Definition:** The period within which the seller must accept or reject the offer.

- ◆ **Details to Include:** Mention a specific deadline (e.g., 7 days) for the seller to respond to the offer. If the offer is not accepted within this timeframe, it becomes void.

- ◆ **Importance:** Encourages timely decision-making by the seller and protects the buyer from indefinite waiting periods.

15. Assignment Clause

- **Definition:** Indicates whether the buyer has the right to assign the agreement to another party.
- **Details to Include:** Clarify if the buyer can assign or transfer their interest in the property to another individual or entity.
- **Importance:** Provides flexibility to the buyer in case of unforeseen circumstances.

Summary

Drafting a Comprehensive Offer Including these key terms in your offer ensures that the agreement is comprehensive, transparent, and legally sound. It protects both parties and provides a clear framework for completing the transaction. It's always advisable to consult with a real estate agent or legal expert when drafting an offer to ensure that all local regulations and legal requirements are met.

HANDLING COUNTEROFFERS AND NEGOTIATION TACTICS

Handling counteroffers and employing effective negotiation tactics are crucial steps in successfully purchasing a home in India. The negotiation phase often begins after you make an initial offer and the seller responds with a counteroffer. Knowing how to handle these situations strategically can help you secure the property at a fair price and with favourable terms.

Handling Counteroffers in India

When a seller responds to your initial offer with a counteroffer, it typically means they are interested in selling but want to negotiate on certain terms, such as the price, payment schedule, closing date, or other contingencies. Here's how to handle counteroffers effectively:

1. Understand the Seller's Motivations

- **Assess the Counteroffer:** Carefully review the counteroffer to understand which terms the seller wants to change. Is the seller primarily focused on price, or are they more concerned about the timing of payments, possession dates, or other conditions?

- **Gauge Seller's Urgency:** Determine the seller's urgency or motivation to sell. For example, if the seller needs to relocate quickly or is under financial pressure, they might be more flexible in other areas.

2. Decide on Your Next Move

- **Accept the Counteroffer:** If the counteroffer is within your budget and meets your primary conditions, you can accept it. Make sure to get this acceptance in writing to avoid misunderstandings.

- **Counter the Counteroffer:** If the counteroffer is not acceptable, consider countering it with a revised offer. This could involve meeting the seller halfway on the price, adjusting contingencies, or proposing different terms.

- **Reject the Counteroffer:** If the seller's terms are far from what you are willing or able to accept, you might choose to reject the counteroffer. Ensure you communicate this politely, leaving the door open for further negotiation if the seller reconsiders.

3. Prioritize Your Terms

- **Identify Non-Negotiables:** Clearly define which aspects of the offer are non-negotiable for you (e.g., maximum budget, property condition, closing date).

- **Be Flexible on Other Terms:** While sticking to your non-negotiables, show flexibility in other areas where you can compromise. For example, you might offer to adjust the possession date to align with the seller's preferences.

4. Maintain Open Communication

- **Be Transparent:** Clearly communicate your needs and expectations to the seller or their agent. Transparency can help build trust and encourage a collaborative approach to finding common ground.

- **Use an Intermediary:** If negotiations become tense, consider using a real estate agent or legal professional to mediate. An intermediary can offer unbiased advice and help maintain a constructive dialogue.

5. Know When to Walk Away

- **Set a Walk-Away Point:** Know your limits and be prepared to walk away if the negotiations are not moving in your favour or if the terms exceed your budget or comfort level.

- **Avoid Emotional Decisions:** Don't let emotions drive your decisions. Focus on the financial and practical aspects of the deal.

Negotiation Tactics for Home Buying in India

Effective negotiation tactics can help you get the best deal while maintaining a positive relationship with the seller. Here are some tactics tailored to the Indian real estate market:

1. Do Your Homework

- **Market Research:** Gather data on recent sales of similar properties in the area to understand the fair market value. This information will strengthen your position when negotiating on price.

- **Property-Specific Research:** Understand the history and condition of the property. Know about any legal issues, pending approvals, or disputes that may affect its value. Use this information to your advantage during negotiations.

2. Start with a Reasonable Offer

- **Avoid Lowball Offers:** While it's essential to start negotiations lower than your maximum budget, avoid making an offer that is too low. A lowball offer can offend the seller and close the door to further negotiations.

- **Offer Just Below Your Budget:** Start with an offer slightly below your maximum budget to allow room for negotiation. This shows the seller that you are serious while giving you flexibility to negotiate up.

3. Use Market Conditions to Your Advantage

- **Buyer's Market Tactic:** In a buyer's market (where supply exceeds demand), highlight market data that supports your lower offer, such as declining property prices, high inventory levels, or longer listing times.

- **Seller's Market Tactic:** In a seller's market (where demand exceeds supply), be prepared to make a stronger initial offer and include favourable terms (like a quicker closing date) to make your offer stand out among multiple buyers.

4. Highlight Your Strength as a Buyer

- **Pre-Approval Advantage:** Show that you have a pre-approved home loan, which demonstrates your financial readiness and commitment to purchasing.

- **Cash Buyer Tactic:** If you are a cash buyer, emphasize this advantage. Cash offers are often more attractive to sellers because they avoid financing contingencies and speed up the closing process.

5. Be Willing to Compromise

- **Focus on Win-Win Outcomes:** Aim for a win-win negotiation where both parties feel satisfied with the outcome. For example, if the seller is adamant about the price, ask for other concessions like repairs, a longer closing period, or included fixtures.

- **Be Creative with Terms:** Offer flexibility on aspects like the closing date, payment schedule, or possession timing. This can make your offer more attractive without altering the purchase price.

6. Leverage Inspection Results

- **Use Home Inspection Findings:** If the inspection reveals any issues (e.g., structural problems, electrical faults, plumbing leaks), use this as leverage to negotiate a lower price or request repairs before closing.

- **Ask for Concessions:** Instead of lowering the price, you can ask for the seller to cover certain closing costs, provide a home warranty, or include specific appliances or fixtures.

7. Understand Cultural Nuances

- **Respect and Politeness:** In India, maintaining respect and politeness is critical. Approach negotiations with a calm, respectful demeanour to build rapport with the seller.

- **Indirect Negotiation Tactics:** Sometimes, sellers may not be direct about their concerns or expectations. Pay attention to indirect cues and be prepared to read between the lines.

8. Use Deadlines to Your Advantage

- **Create a Sense of Urgency:** If you are confident in your offer, set a deadline for the seller to respond. This can create a sense of urgency and prevent prolonged negotiations.

- **Avoid Tight Deadlines in a Seller's Market:** If the market is hot and competitive, avoid setting tight deadlines that could put off the seller. Be patient and allow reasonable time for a response.

9. Be Prepared for Multiple Rounds

- **Anticipate Counteroffers:** Expect multiple rounds of counteroffers, especially in a competitive market. Be ready to reassess and adjust your offer based on the seller's feedback.

- **Stay Firm on Critical Terms:** While showing flexibility, stay firm on your non-negotiable terms (e.g., maximum budget or specific contingencies).

10. Build Rapport and Trust

- **Find Common Ground:** If possible, find common ground with the seller. Building a personal connection can create goodwill and make negotiations smoother.

- **Use an Experienced Real Estate Agent:** An experienced real estate agent familiar with local market conditions and cultural nuances can guide you through negotiations and improve your chances of a favourable outcome.

Summary: Navigating Counteroffers and Negotiations

Negotiating effectively involves a blend of preparation, strategy, and adaptability. By understanding the seller's motivations, conducting thorough research, and employing a mix of tactics, you can navigate counteroffers successfully and achieve a favourable outcome. Remember that negotiation is a process—stay patient, keep your goals in focus, and remain open to compromise to secure the best deal for your new home in India.

WHEN TO WALK AWAY: RECOGNIZING DEAL BREAKER

Recognizing deal breakers and knowing when to walk away from a property transaction in India is crucial for making a sound financial decision. Not every deal will be a good fit, and understanding when to step back can save you from potential headaches, legal issues, and financial loss.

When to Walk Away: Recognizing Deal Breakers in India

Here are some key deal breakers to look out for when buying a home in India:

1. Legal Complications with the Property Title

- **Red Flags:** If the property has an unclear or disputed title, or if there are multiple claims to ownership, this is a significant deal breaker. Other legal issues may include pending litigation, unregistered property, or lack of government approvals.

- **Reason to Walk Away:** A property with legal complications can lead to lengthy legal battles, unexpected costs, and even the risk of losing the property. It's essential to ensure that the property has a clean, marketable title with all necessary approvals.

2. Encumbrances and Liens

- **Red Flags:** If the property is mortgaged or has unpaid dues like property taxes, utility bills, or maintenance charges, it may have encumbrances or liens against it.

- **Reason to Walk Away:** Encumbrances can delay the transfer of ownership and may require you to pay off these debts. Always conduct an encumbrance check at the Sub-Registrar's office or consult with a legal expert to verify the property's status.

3. Non-Compliance with Regulatory Approvals

- **Red Flags:** If the property lacks necessary approvals from authorities like the Real Estate Regulatory Authority (RERA), municipal corporation, or local development authority, it could be a deal breaker. Look out for issues like illegal construction, unauthorized land use, or lack of occupancy certificates.

- **Reason to Walk Away:** Non-compliance can lead to hefty penalties, demolition, or legal action by authorities. Always verify that the property complies with local building codes and regulations.

4. Poor Quality of Construction

- **Red Flags:** Signs of poor construction quality, such as visible cracks in walls, dampness, plumbing leaks, electrical faults, or substandard materials, are significant deal breakers. Also, be cautious if the property is in a flood-prone area or has a history of structural issues.

- **Reason to Walk Away:** Poor construction quality can result in high maintenance costs, frequent repairs, and potential safety hazards. A property in a poor state may not provide a good return on investment or a safe living environment.

5. Unrealistic Pricing or Overvalued Property

- **Red Flags:** If the property is priced significantly higher than comparable properties in the area, it may be overvalued. Unrealistic pricing can also be indicated by a seller who refuses to negotiate or adjust the price based on market trends.

- **Reason to Walk Away:** Overpaying for a property can affect your financial health and reduce your chances of making a profit in the future. Always conduct a comparative market analysis to assess whether the price aligns with the market rate.

6. Unfavourable Financing Terms

- **Red Flags:** If the lender offers unfavourable loan terms, such as high interest rates, short repayment periods, or excessive processing fees, it could be a deal breaker. Inadequate pre-approval or delays in obtaining financing are also warning signs.

- **Reason to Walk Away:** Unfavourable financing can strain your finances and increase your overall cost of ownership. Compare different financing options and ensure the terms are suitable for your budget and long-term financial goals.

7. Seller's Unwillingness to Negotiate or Disclose Information

- **Red Flags:** If the seller is unwilling to negotiate on price, repairs, or contingencies, or refuses to provide necessary documentation (e.g., title deeds, building approvals, property tax receipts), it could indicate a problem.

- **Reason to Walk Away:** Lack of transparency or unwillingness to negotiate can suggest that the seller is hiding something or that they do not genuinely intend to sell under fair terms. Trustworthy transactions require openness and flexibility from both parties.

8. Negative Inspection Reports

- **Red Flags:** If a professional home inspection reveals significant issues such as termite infestations, Mold, structural damage, faulty wiring, or plumbing problems, it is a deal breaker.

- **Reason to Walk Away:** Major defects can lead to costly repairs and could affect the property's habitability. If the seller refuses to fix these issues or provide compensation, walking away may be the best option.

9. Unreasonable Contingencies and Clauses

- **Red Flags:** If the purchase agreement contains unreasonable contingencies, such as extensive seller conditions, no refund of earnest money in any situation, or unclear terms regarding possession and payments, consider it a red flag.

- **Reason to Walk Away:** Unreasonable contingencies can put you at risk of losing your deposit or create legal and financial complications. Always seek legal advice before signing any agreement with ambiguous or biased clauses.

10. Unfavourable Location or Future Development Plans

- **Red Flags:** If the property is in a location with poor infrastructure, inadequate public transport, high crime rates, or is subject to adverse future developments (e.g., highways, factories, or commercial complexes), it may not be a good investment.

- **Reason to Walk Away:** The location significantly affects property value and liveability. If future developments or current conditions do not align with your lifestyle or investment goals, it is better to look elsewhere.

11. Misalignment with Your Long-Term Goals

- **Red Flags:** If the property does not align with your long-term goals—whether it's living in the property, renting it out, or reselling it at a profit—this is a deal breaker.

- **Reason to Walk Away:** A property should meet your needs and financial goals. If it doesn't align with your vision or future plans, continuing with the purchase could lead to regret.

12. Poor Resale Potential

- **Red Flags:** Indicators of poor resale potential include a declining neighborhood, high inventory levels, or low demand for properties in the area.

- **Reason to Walk Away:** A property with poor resale potential can affect your ability to recoup your investment or achieve financial growth. Always consider the future marketability of the property.

13. Compromised Amenities and Infrastructure

- **Red Flags:** Lack of essential amenities (such as water supply, electricity, and waste management) or poor infrastructure (e.g., roads, schools, hospitals) can be significant deal breakers.

- **Reason to Walk Away:** Compromised amenities and infrastructure can impact your quality of life and reduce the property's attractiveness to future buyers or tenants.

14. Negative Feedback from Neighbours or Local Community

- Red Flags: Negative feedback from neighbours or the local community about safety, noise, pollution, or developer reputation can indicate potential issues.

- Reason to Walk Away: Local insights can provide valuable information about a property's liveability and desirability. Consider this feedback seriously before proceeding.

Summary: Knowing When to Walk Away

Buying a home in India is a significant investment, and recognizing these deal breakers can help you make a well-informed decision. Trust your instincts and be prepared to walk away if any red flags arise. It's always better to err on the side of caution than to rush into a problematic deal.

If you are ever unsure about whether to proceed with a purchase, consult with a real estate expert or legal professional to review the terms and conditions thoroughly.

CHAPTER 7

SECURING FINANCING AND CLOSING DEAL

Finalizing your mortgage application in India is a crucial step in the home-buying process. It requires careful attention to detail, coordination with your lender, and ensuring that all necessary documentation is in place. Here's a comprehensive guide to help you successfully finalize your mortgage application:

Steps to Finalize Your Mortgage Application in India

1. Review Your Loan Offer Letter

Once your mortgage application is pre-approved, your lender will issue a **Loan Offer Letter** outlining the terms and conditions of the loan. This is a critical document that you must thoroughly review before accepting.

- **Key Elements to Check:**
  - Loan amount approved
  - Interest rate (fixed or floating)
  - Loan tenure
  - EMI (Equated Monthly Instalments)
  - Processing fees and other charges
  - Prepayment and foreclosure terms
  - Any other special conditions
- **Next Steps:** If you are satisfied with the terms, sign and return the offer letter to the bank. If you have any doubts or wish to negotiate better terms, contact your lender for clarification or renegotiation.

2. Submit All Required Documentation

Lenders in India require several documents to verify your eligibility and finalize the mortgage. Make sure you gather and submit all necessary paperwork as soon as possible. Incomplete documentation can delay the loan approval process.

- **Commonly Required Documents:**
  - **Identity Proof:** Aadhaar Card, Passport, PAN Card, Voter ID
  - **Address Proof:** Utility bills, Passport, Aadhaar Card, Ration Card
  - **Income Proof:**
    - Salaried individuals: Salary slips (last 3-6 months), Form 16, bank statements
    - Self-employed individuals: IT returns (last 2-3 years), business financials, profit & loss statements
  - **Property Documents:**
    - Sale agreement
    - Title deeds
    - Approved building plan
    - NOC (No Objection Certificate) from the builder or society
    - Encumbrance certificate
  - **Employment Proof:** Employment letter, work experience certificate (for salaried applicants)
  - **Other Documents:**
    - Passport-size photographs
    - Legal property valuation report (provided by bank-approved valuers)
- **Next Steps:** Ensure that all documents are up to date, signed where necessary, and submitted in the required format. Double-check all details to avoid rejection or delays.

3. Property Verification and Legal Check

Once the lender receives your documents, they will initiate the **legal and technical verification** of the property. This is to ensure that the property has a clear title and meets the bank's standards for disbursing a loan.

- **Legal Verification:**
  - ◆ A legal expert (appointed by the lender) will verify the property's title deeds to ensure that it is free from encumbrances and that the seller has the legal right to transfer the ownership.
  - ◆ They will also check for disputes or litigation associated with the property.
- **Technical Verification:**
  - ◆ A property valuer or surveyor (appointed by the bank) will visit the property for an inspection. They will check the physical condition, layout, and construction status of the property.
  - ◆ The valuer will also assess whether the property's market value matches the loan amount.
- **Next Steps:** Be prepared to provide additional documents if requested by the bank's legal and technical teams. Once the property is approved, the loan moves to the next stage.

4. Pay the Processing Fees

After successful verification, the lender will ask you to pay the **processing fee** to proceed with the loan disbursal. Processing fees typically range between 0.5% to 2% of the loan amount, depending on the bank and loan product.

- **Next Steps:** Make the payment and keep a receipt for future reference. Some banks may offer to deduct this from the loan amount, but it's important to clarify how the fee will be handled.

5. Loan Sanction and Agreement Signing

Once the processing fee is paid and the lender is satisfied with all verifications, the loan will be **sanctioned**. At this point, the lender will prepare the **Loan Agreement**, which includes all the terms and conditions that will govern the mortgage.

- **Next Steps:**
  - ◆ **Read the Loan Agreement Thoroughly:** Ensure you understand all clauses related to repayment, prepayment, foreclosure charges, late payment penalties, and other conditions.
  - ◆ **Sign the Agreement:** If everything is in order, sign the agreement in the presence of the bank's representatives.

6. Choose Your EMI Plan

Depending on your financial situation, you can choose an EMI plan that suits you best. Most banks offer the following options:

- **Step-Up EMI Plan:** This allows you to pay lower EMIs in the initial years and increase payments gradually as your income rises.

- **Step-Down EMI Plan:** You can start with higher EMIs and reduce them over time.

- **Balloon EMI Plan:** This plan allows you to pay smaller EMIs throughout the loan tenure, with a lump-sum payment at the end.

- **Next Steps:** Discuss your financial goals with the bank and choose a plan that fits your long-term affordability.

7. Loan Disbursement

After the agreement is signed and the EMI plan is finalized, the bank will disburse the loan. Disbursement can either be **full** or **partial**, depending on the stage of construction of the property or the terms agreed upon.

- **Full Disbursement:** In case of a ready-to-move property, the entire loan amount will be disbursed at once.

- **Partial Disbursement:** For under-construction properties, the loan amount is disbursed in phases, as per the construction progress.

- **Next Steps:**
  - **Disbursement to Seller/Builder:** The bank will directly transfer the amount to the seller or builder as per the sale agreement terms.

  - **Commencement of EMI:** Once the loan is disbursed, EMI payments will start from the next month. Keep track of the EMI due date and make sure sufficient funds are in your account.

8. Keep Track of Post-Disbursement Formalities

- **Loan Account Information:** After disbursement, the bank will set up your loan account. You will receive loan account details, including the loan number, EMI schedule, and repayment method.

- **Loan Statements:** Periodically review loan statements to monitor your payments and interest accrual. Most banks offer online access to loan account information.

- **Interest Rate Monitoring:** If you have opted for a **floating interest rate**, keep an eye on market trends. If interest rates drop, you might benefit from refinancing or negotiating with the bank for lower rates.

- **Next Steps:** Be proactive in tracking your loan account and make sure you understand any changes in interest rates or EMI schedules.

Common Mistakes to Avoid When Finalizing Your Mortgage Application

- **Rushing the Process:** Don't rush into signing the loan agreement without fully understanding the terms and conditions.

- **Not Comparing Loan Offers:** While you may have already received pre-approval, it's still a good idea to compare different loan products from other banks before finalizing.

- **Ignoring Hidden Fees:** Ensure you understand all the fees involved in the loan, including processing fees, legal charges, and foreclosure penalties.

- **Overstretching Budget:** Be realistic about the loan amount and EMI payments. Stretching your budget too thin can lead to financial stress down the line.

Summary: Finalizing Your Mortgage Application

Finalizing your mortgage application in India involves a series of steps, from reviewing the loan offer and submitting necessary documents to signing the loan agreement and disbursing the loan. Each step requires careful attention to detail and a thorough understanding of the terms and conditions. By staying organized, proactive, and well-informed, you can ensure a smooth home loan process.

UNDERSTANDING THE CLOSING COSTS AND FEES

Closing costs and fees are the various expenses associated with finalizing the purchase of a home and securing a mortgage. In India, these costs can significantly add to the overall expenses of buying a home, and understanding them is crucial for financial planning.

Here's a detailed guide to understanding closing costs and fees in India:

1. Stamp Duty

- **What It Is:** Stamp duty is a government tax paid on the transaction of property. The rate varies from state to state and is usually between **5% to 8%** of the property's sale value or circle rate, whichever is higher.

- **Why It's Important:** Stamp duty legalizes the property purchase agreement and makes it enforceable in a court of law.

- **Who Pays:** Typically, the buyer pays the stamp duty.

Tip: Some states offer lower stamp duty rates for women buyers, so it may be worth considering registering the property in the name of a female family member.

2. Registration Fees

- **What It Is:** This is the fee for registering the property in your name with the local sub-registrar's office. It's usually **1% of the property value**.

- **Why It's Important:** Registration is mandatory to officially transfer the ownership of the property from the seller to the buyer.

- **Who Pays:** The buyer pays the registration fee.

3. GST (Goods and Services Tax)

- **What It Is:** GST is applicable on the purchase of under-construction properties, but not on fully constructed and ready-to-move properties. The current GST rate is **5% for residential properties** and **1% for affordable housing**.

- **Why It's Important:** If you're buying a property that's under construction, GST will add to your costs.

- **Who Pays:** The buyer pays GST on the property's base price.

4. Home Loan Processing Fees

- **What It Is:** This fee is charged by the lender for processing your home loan application. It usually ranges between **0.5% to 2% of the loan amount.**

- **Why It's Important:** The processing fee covers administrative expenses like verifying your documentation, legal checks, and valuation of the property.

- **Who Pays:** The borrower (homebuyer) pays the processing fee.

Tip: Some banks and housing finance companies may offer discounts or waive processing fees during promotional periods. It's worth exploring these options.

5. Legal Fees

- **What It Is:** Legal fees are paid to a lawyer who reviews the property's title, ensures there are no legal disputes, and verifies the legality of the transaction.

- **Why It's Important:** Having a clean and legally verified title is crucial to avoid future litigation or ownership disputes.

- **Who Pays:** The buyer usually bears the legal fees.

- **Approximate Cost:** Legal fees vary based on the complexity of the property deal but are generally between ₹10,000 to ₹50,000.

6. Title Search Charges

- **What It Is:** These charges are for conducting a **title search** to verify the property's ownership history and to ensure there are no outstanding loans, encumbrances, or disputes.

- **Why It's Important:** A thorough title search ensures you're purchasing a property with a clear title, reducing the risk of future legal complications.

- **Who Pays:** The buyer or lender may bear this cost.

- **Approximate Cost:** Typically around ₹5,000 to ₹20,000 depending on the property's location and complexity.

7. Valuation Charges

- **What It Is:** Property valuation charges are paid to a bank-approved valuer to assess the market value of the property.

- **Why It's Important:** The valuation report helps determine whether the property's market value aligns with the loan amount.

- **Who Pays:** Usually the buyer or the lender (the bank may include this as part of processing fees).

- **Approximate Cost:** Valuation charges are generally between ₹5,000 to ₹15,000.

8. Maintenance Deposit (for Apartments)

- **What It Is:** When purchasing an apartment, you may need to pay an upfront maintenance deposit to the developer or society for building upkeep and maintenance. This is usually collected for **1 to 5 years in advance**.

- **Why It's Important:** This deposit ensures the building's common areas are maintained and repairs are handled without delay.

- **Who Pays:** The buyer pays this deposit.

- **Approximate Cost:** The amount varies but is usually around ₹25,000 to ₹2,00,000, depending on the apartment's size and amenities.

9. Brokerage Fees

- **What It Is:** If you hire a real estate broker or agent to help you find a property, you will need to pay a brokerage fee, which is typically **1% to 2% of the property's sale value**.

- **Why It's Important:** Brokers facilitate the buying process by showing you properties, handling negotiations, and assisting with paperwork.

- **Who Pays:** The buyer usually pays the brokerage fee, though in some cases the seller may split the fee.

10. Pre-EMI Interest

- **What It Is:** If you've taken a home loan for an under-construction property, you may be required to pay **Pre-EMI interest** until the property is ready for possession. Pre-EMI is the interest on the loan amount disbursed, but without any principal repayment.

- **Why It's Important:** Pre-EMI reduces the immediate financial burden but adds to the overall interest cost.
- **Who Pays:** The borrower pays Pre-EMI interest to the lender.

11. Insurance Costs

- **What It Is:** Lenders may require you to take **home loan insurance** or **property insurance** to safeguard the loan and the property.
- **Why It's Important:** Home loan insurance protects your family from the burden of repaying the loan in case of unforeseen events like death or disability. Property insurance covers damages to the property.
- **Who Pays:** The buyer pays the insurance premium.
- **Approximate Cost:** The cost of home loan insurance is typically **0.2% to 0.5% of the loan amount per year**, and property insurance costs depend on the property's value.

12. Miscellaneous Costs

Other small but significant costs may include:

- **Notary Charges:** If certain documents need to be notarized, this fee can range from ₹500 to ₹5,000.
- **Franking Charges:** Applicable for stamping certain loan or sale documents, generally **0.1% of the loan amount**.
- **Society Transfer Charges:** When buying a resale property in a housing society, you may need to pay a society transfer fee. This can range from ₹10,000 to ₹50,000, depending on the society's rules.

Total Estimate of Closing Costs in India

The total closing costs generally range between **7% to 10% of the property value**, depending on factors like the state's stamp duty rates, the type of property, and the loan amount. These costs can add up, so it's essential to budget for them early in the home-buying process.

How to Plan for Closing Costs

1. **Budget Early:** Include closing costs in your overall financial planning for buying a home. These can be significant and should not be overlooked.

2. **Negotiate Where Possible:** Some fees like legal fees, brokerage, or even loan processing fees can sometimes be negotiated.

3. **Keep Funds Readily Available:** Closing costs are often paid upfront, so make sure you have liquid funds ready when it's time to finalize the purchase.

Summary

Understanding and planning for closing costs is a critical aspect of buying a home in India. While they may seem overwhelming, being aware of these costs in advance will help you better prepare for the final stages of home buying. From government fees like stamp duty and registration to bank charges like processing fees, ensuring that you're financially ready for all closing costs can make your home-buying experience smoother.

PREPARING FOR CLOSING DAY: WHAT TO EXPECT

Closing day is the final step in the home-buying process, where all legalities are completed, ownership of the property is transferred, and you officially become a homeowner. In India, preparing for closing day involves several key tasks, documents, and steps. Here's a comprehensive guide to help you understand what to expect and how to prepare.

1. Pre-Closing Checklist: Key Preparations

Before closing day, ensure the following tasks are completed:

- **Final Loan Approval:** Confirm that your home loan is fully approved, and you have signed the loan agreement with the bank.

- **Property Documentation:** Ensure all the legal and property documents (sale deed, title documents, encumbrance certificates, etc.) have been verified and are ready.

- **Legal Verification:** Make sure your lawyer has verified the property's legal status and there are no pending disputes, dues, or encumbrances.

- **Final Property Inspection:** Conduct a final walkthrough or inspection of the property to ensure that everything is in order (especially for under-construction properties).

- **Funds:** Ensure that you have the necessary funds available for down payment, closing costs, and any other required payments.

- **Power of Attorney (if needed):** If you are unable to be physically present on closing day, you may need to issue a Power of Attorney (PoA) to someone you trust to sign documents on your behalf.

2. Key Documents for Closing Day

On closing day, there are several critical documents that need to be signed and submitted to complete the transfer of ownership. Here are the key documents to have ready:

A. Sale Deed

- **What It Is:** The Sale Deed is the most important document for transferring ownership from the seller to the buyer. It outlines the terms of the sale and confirms the seller's legal right to sell the property.

- **Who Prepares It:** Usually, the buyer's or seller's lawyer prepares the Sale Deed, and it is executed at the local sub-registrar's office.

- **Significance:** The sale deed is the document that officially transfers ownership from the seller to the buyer.

B. Title Documents

- **What It Is:** These are documents that establish the seller's legal right to transfer the property and prove the property's ownership history.

- **Examples Include:**
  - Mother deed
  - Chain of title documents
  - Encumbrance certificate (which shows that the property is free of any financial or legal liabilities)

- **Why It's Important:** Title documents ensure that the property has a clear and marketable title.

C. Loan Agreement and Mortgage Documents

- **What It Is:** If you are financing the purchase through a home loan, the bank will require you to sign the final loan agreement and mortgage documents.

- **Why It's Important:** These documents outline the terms of the loan, including repayment schedules, interest rates, and penalties for late payments.

- **Who Prepares It:** The lender (bank) prepares these documents.

D. Payment Receipts

- **What It Is:** Payment receipts provide proof of the payments made by the buyer to the seller and any other parties (e.g., brokers, builders, etc.). These include:
  - Down payment receipt
  - Stamp duty and registration fee payment receipts

- **Why It's Important:** These receipts will be needed for future reference and are required by the sub-registrar's office to process the registration of the property.

E. No Objection Certificate (NOC)

- **What It Is:** If you're purchasing a property in a housing society or a building, the seller should provide a No Objection Certificate (NOC) from the society or developer.

- **Why It's Important:** The NOC ensures that the society or builder has no objections to transferring the property and that there are no outstanding dues (e.g., maintenance fees).

3. Registration of the Property

The registration of the Sale Deed at the **sub-registrar's office** is one of the most important steps on closing day. Here's what to expect during the registration process:

A. Stamp Duty and Registration Fees

- **Stamp Duty:** Ensure that you have paid the applicable stamp duty, which is typically 5% to 8% of the property value.

- **Registration Fees:** The registration fee, usually 1% of the property value, also needs to be paid before registering the Sale Deed.

- **Payment Proof:** Keep the payment receipts for both the stamp duty and registration fees handy, as they will be needed during the registration process.

B. Document Execution

- Both the buyer and the seller, along with two witnesses, will need to be physically present at the sub-registrar's office to sign the Sale Deed.

- After signing, the Sale Deed is submitted for registration with the sub-registrar.

- Once the Sale Deed is registered, the property is officially transferred to your name.

C. Biometric Verification

- Most states in India now require biometric verification of the buyer, seller, and witnesses during the registration process.

- This is done to prevent fraud and ensure the identity of all parties involved.

4. Payment and Disbursement

A. Final Payments

- **Balance Payment to Seller:** Ensure that the final payment, as per the sale agreement, is ready to be disbursed to the seller on closing day.

- **Down Payment:** Ensure that the down payment (if not already paid) is made on closing day.

- **Closing Costs:** Closing costs such as legal fees, stamp duty, registration fees, etc., should be paid on or before closing day.

B. Loan Disbursement

- If you are taking a home loan, the bank will disburse the loan amount to the seller or builder after you sign the loan agreement.

- If the property is under construction, the bank may disburse the amount in phases, as per the construction stage.

5. Post-Closing Steps

A. Obtain Registered Sale Deed

- After the registration is completed, the sub-registrar's office will provide a **registered copy of the Sale Deed**, which is the legal proof of ownership.

- Keep the registered Sale Deed in a safe place, as it will be required for any future transactions or legal issues.

B. Mutation of Property

- **What It Is:** Mutation is the process of updating the property records (in the local municipality or revenue department) in the buyer's name.

- **Why It's Important:** It's important for taxation purposes and to establish legal ownership of the property in government records.

- **How to Do It:** Submit a copy of the registered Sale Deed along with an application for mutation at the local municipality office.

C. Loan Repayment Begins

- Once the loan is disbursed, your **EMIs (Equated Monthly Instalments)** will start as per the loan agreement.
- Ensure that your bank account is funded adequately for the automatic EMI deductions to avoid penalties.

6. Common Challenges on Closing Day

- **Delays at the Sub-Registrar's Office:** Delays can occur due to long queues or system issues at the sub-registrar's office. Be prepared for a potential wait.
- **Documentation Issues:** If any documents are incomplete or missing, it could delay the registration process.
- **Final Payment Issues:** Ensure that your bank accounts have sufficient funds for payments like stamp duty, registration fees, and the final settlement with the seller.

7. Celebrating the Closing

After completing the closing process and receiving the keys to your new home, it's time to celebrate! You are now officially a homeowner. Be sure to keep all documents organized for future reference, and start planning your move or the next steps for your property.

Summary

Closing day in India is the culmination of the home-buying process, involving legal formalities, documentation, and financial transactions. By understanding what to expect and preparing in advance, you can ensure a smooth closing experience. From signing the Sale Deed and registering the property to disbursing final payments and securing a loan, this day marks the official transfer of ownership and the start of your journey as a homeowner.

REVIEWING FINAL DOCUMENTS AND SIGNING THE PAPERS

Reviewing and signing the final documents is one of the most important steps in the home-buying process in India. On closing day, several legal documents need to be thoroughly reviewed, understood, and signed to finalize the transfer of ownership and ensure all legalities are in place.

Here's a comprehensive guide to reviewing and signing the final papers in India:

1. Sale Deed

What It Is:

- The **Sale Deed** is the primary legal document that officially transfers ownership of the property from the seller to the buyer. It contains details about the property, the transaction, and the terms and conditions agreed upon by both parties.

What to Check:

- **Buyer and Seller Details:** Ensure that your and the seller's names and identification details are accurate.

- **Property Description:** Verify that the property's full description, including its boundaries, location, and any fixtures, is correct.

- **Sale Consideration (Price):** Confirm that the property's sale price matches the agreed-upon amount in the agreement.

- **Payment Details:** Check if all payments, including the down payment and remaining balance, are mentioned along with the mode of payment (bank transfer, cheque, etc.).

- **Possession Date:** Ensure that the possession date, when you are entitled to take control of the property, is clearly mentioned.

- **Signature Lines:** Both parties, the buyer and the seller, need to sign the document. Ensure there is space for the signatures of both, along with two witnesses.

Why It's Important:

- The sale deed is crucial because it serves as the legal proof of ownership. Without a properly executed and registered sale deed, you cannot claim legal ownership of the property.

2. Title Deed

What It Is:

- The **Title Deed** certifies the seller's ownership of the property and their right to sell it. It traces the ownership history and ensures the property has a clear and marketable title.

What to Check:

- **Ownership History:** Verify the chain of ownership to ensure there are no disputes or ambiguities.

- **Encumbrance:** Confirm there are no encumbrances (like mortgages or liens) on the property.

- **Clear Title:** The property should have a clear title, meaning there are no legal disputes or third-party claims.

Why It's Important:

- A title deed ensures that the seller has a legal right to sell the property. It protects you from future legal disputes regarding ownership.

3. Loan Agreement and Mortgage Documents (if applicable)

What It Is:

- If you're purchasing the property with a home loan, the **Loan Agreement** outlines the terms and conditions of the loan, including the interest rate, tenure, EMI, and penalties for defaults.

- **Mortgage Documents** transfer a security interest in the property to the lender until the loan is repaid.

What to Check:

- **Loan Terms:** Double-check the interest rate (fixed or variable), loan tenure, and EMI amounts to ensure they align with what you agreed to with the lender.

- **Prepayment and Penalties:** Review the terms for prepayment or foreclosure, and understand the penalties for delayed payments.

- **Mortgage Clauses:** Verify the mortgage clauses, including the lender's rights over the property in case of default.

- **Signature Requirements:** Ensure you sign the loan agreement, and if needed, have any guarantors sign as well.

Why It's Important:

- The loan agreement formalizes your commitment to repay the loan. Understanding your repayment obligations and the lender's rights will prevent future financial strain.

4. NOC (No Objection Certificate)

What It Is:

A **No Objection Certificate (NOC)** is issued by the housing society, builder, or other relevant authorities to confirm that they have no objections to the sale and transfer of the property to the buyer.

- It ensures that all dues, like maintenance or utility bills, are cleared by the seller.

What to Check:

- **No Outstanding Dues:** Ensure that the NOC confirms there are no outstanding dues, such as maintenance fees, utility bills, or any unpaid loans.

- **Transfer of Ownership Approval:** Verify that the NOC clearly states approval for the transfer of ownership to your name.

Why It's Important:

- The NOC ensures that you won't be held liable for any unpaid bills or obligations of the seller after the transfer.

5. Encumbrance Certificate (EC)

What It Is:

- An **Encumbrance Certificate (EC)** is a document that provides proof that the property is free from any legal or financial liabilities such as loans or disputes.

What to Check:

- **No Encumbrances:** Ensure that the EC, obtained from the sub-registrar's office, shows a **nil encumbrance** for the period of at least 13-30 years.

- **Verification by Lawyer:** Have your lawyer verify the EC to ensure the property is free from any financial burdens.

Why It's Important:

- The EC protects you from acquiring a property that might have unpaid loans or legal claims attached to it.

6. Payment Receipts

What It Is:

- These are receipts confirming the payments you have made to the seller and other relevant parties (e.g., stamp duty, registration fees, etc.).

What to Check:

- **Down Payment Receipt:** Ensure the seller provides a receipt for the down payment.

- **Stamp Duty and Registration Fees:** Keep the receipts for these payments as they are required for the registration of the property.

- **Loan Disbursement Receipt:** If the home loan has been disbursed, ensure you have the lender's acknowledgment of the payment made to the seller.

Why It's Important:

- Proper receipts act as proof that you've fulfilled your financial obligations and are required for tax and legal purposes.

7. Power of Attorney (if applicable)

What It Is:

- If either the buyer or seller is unable to be present for the signing, a **Power of Attorney (PoA)** allows a designated person to act on their behalf to sign documents and complete the transaction.

What to Check:

- **Legal Validity:** Ensure that the Power of Attorney document is legally valid, notarized, and registered.

- **Specific Powers:** Verify that the PoA grants the holder the specific authority to complete the property transaction.

Why It's Important:

- If you're relying on someone else to sign the documents, having a valid Power of Attorney ensures the transaction is legally binding.

8. Final Property Inspection Report (if applicable)

What It Is:

- This is a document prepared by a property inspector or an engineer that verifies the physical condition of the property at the time of sale.

What to Check:

- **Property Condition:** Ensure the property is in the agreed-upon condition and matches the specifications provided by the seller or developer.

- **No Pending Repairs:** Verify that any agreed-upon repairs or fixes have been completed.

Why It's Important:

- This report prevents post-purchase disputes regarding the condition of the property.

9. Registration Documents

What It Is:

- The final step in the sale process is registering the Sale Deed at the local sub-registrar's office, which involves paying stamp duty and registration fees.

What to Check:

- **Stamp Duty and Registration Fees Paid:** Ensure you have the receipts for these payments.

- **Sale Deed Registration:** Once the Sale Deed is signed and stamped, it will be registered, officially completing the transfer of ownership.

Why It's Important:

- Registering the Sale Deed is necessary for the legal transfer of ownership, and without it, the transaction is incomplete.

10. Witnesses

What It Is:

- Both parties need to have two witnesses who will sign the Sale Deed and other legal documents.

What to Check:

- Ensure that the witnesses are present and ready to sign the Sale Deed and any other documents on closing day.

Summary

Reviewing and signing the final documents is the most crucial step in ensuring a smooth property purchase in India. Careful attention to details in the Sale Deed, title documents, loan agreement, and NOC can save you from future legal or financial issues. Ensure all documents are verified by a lawyer, and don't hesitate to ask questions if anything is unclear. Once signed and registered, you'll have the peace of mind that your home purchase is legally complete, and you're the rightful owner of the property.

PART 4

MOVING IN AND BEYOND

CHAPTER 8

PREPARING FOR YOUR MOVE

Creating a Moving Plan and Budget

Creating a moving plan and budget in India is a crucial step to ensure a smooth and stress-free transition into your new home. A well-organized plan helps you manage your time, resources, and finances efficiently while avoiding last-minute surprises. Here's a comprehensive guide to help you create a moving plan and budget in India:

1. Start Early and Create a Moving Checklist

A. Timeline for Moving

- **Two Months Before Move:**
  - Start by creating a checklist of tasks that need to be completed before the move.
  - Research moving companies, and begin decluttering your home by sorting items you want to keep, donate, or discard.
  - Notify your landlord (if renting) or tenants about the move.
  - Prepare a moving budget.

- **One Month Before Move:**
  - Finalize the moving company or arrange for a rental truck.
  - Start packing non-essential items (seasonal items, books, etc.).
  - Arrange for essential utility transfers (electricity, gas, water, internet).
  - Notify relevant parties of your address change (banks, employers, insurance, etc.).

- **Two Weeks Before Move:**
  - ◆ Begin packing personal items and essential documents.
  - ◆ Schedule final property inspections.
- **One Week Before Move:**
  - ◆ Confirm all moving arrangements.
  - ◆ Pack the remaining items and essentials.
  - ◆ Clean your old home and hand over the keys if required.

2. Creating a Moving Budget

A. Key Costs to Consider

1. **Packing Materials:**
   - ◆ **Boxes:** Cardboard boxes or reusable plastic bins.
   - ◆ **Bubble Wrap and Cushioning:** For fragile items like glassware, electronics, and valuables.
   - ◆ **Packing Tape and Labels:** For sealing and labeling boxes.
   - ◆ **Cost:** ₹2,000 - ₹5,000 depending on the size of the move.

2. **Moving Company Costs:**
   - ◆ Get quotes from multiple moving companies to compare rates.
   - ◆ Charges depend on the distance, volume of goods, and services required (packing, insurance, unloading).
   - ◆ **Local Move (Within City):** ₹5,000 - ₹20,000.
   - ◆ **Inter-City Move:** ₹10,000 - ₹50,000, depending on distance and volume.

3. **Transportation Costs:**
   - ◆ If you are renting a truck, factor in fuel costs, tolls, and vehicle rental charges.
   - ◆ **Truck Rental and Fuel:** ₹3,000 - ₹15,000, depending on the distance and the size of the truck.

4. **Insurance:**
   - ◆ Consider getting insurance for your belongings during the move, especially if you have valuable or fragile items.
   - ◆ **Cost:** ₹1,000 - ₹5,000 depending on the value of the items insured.

5. **Utility Connection/Disconnection Fees:**
   - Costs to disconnect and reconnect essential utilities like electricity, gas, water, and internet.
   - **Cost:** ₹1,000 - ₹3,000 depending on service providers.

6. **Cleaning Services:**
   - If you need professional cleaning services for your old or new home.
   - **Cost:** ₹1,000 - ₹5,000 depending on the size of the house.

7. **Miscellaneous Expenses:**
   - Unexpected costs like repairs, tips for movers, meals, and temporary accommodation.
   - **Set Aside:** ₹5,000 - ₹10,000 as a contingency fund.

3. Finding and Hiring a Moving Company

A. Researching Moving Companies

- **Get Referrals:** Ask friends, family, or your real estate agent for recommendations.
- **Online Reviews:** Check online reviews and ratings of moving companies.
- **Get Quotes:** Obtain at least three quotes for comparison. Ensure the quote covers packing, transport, insurance, and any special services.
- **Insurance:** Confirm whether the moving company offers insurance for your belongings during transit.

B. Questions to Ask Movers

- Do you provide packing services, or is it an extra charge?
- What kind of materials do you use for packing fragile items?
- What is the insurance policy for any damages or losses?
- How long will the move take, and what are the expected delivery times?
- Are there any additional costs (for stairs, narrow streets, etc.)?

4. Decluttering Before the Move

A. Sorting Your Belongings

- **Keep:** Items you use regularly and will need in your new home.

- **Sell:** Consider selling unwanted furniture, electronics, or appliances through online platforms like OLX, Quickr, or Facebook Marketplace.

- **Donate:** Items like clothes, toys, or books can be donated to local charities or organizations.

- **Discard:** Broken, damaged, or outdated items that are no longer useful.

B. Benefits of Decluttering

- **Reduce Moving Costs:** By minimizing the number of items, you can reduce the weight and volume, leading to lower transportation and packing costs.

- **Fresh Start:** Moving with fewer items allows for a more organized setup in your new home.

5. Packing and Labeling Strategy

A. Pack Smart

- **Start Early:** Begin with non-essential items like books, seasonal clothes, and décor.

- **Room-by-Room Packing:** Pack one room at a time to keep things organized.

- **Label Boxes Clearly:** Use color-coded labels or markers to indicate the room the box belongs to (e.g., kitchen, bedroom).

- **Pack Fragile Items Separately:** Use bubble wrap or old newspapers for breakables like glassware, electronics, and art pieces.

B. Essentials Box

- Pack a box with essentials you'll need immediately at your new home, such as toiletries, a change of clothes, snacks, important documents, medications, and basic kitchen items (plates, cutlery).

6. Managing Utilities and Services

A. Transferring Utilities

- Notify your utility providers (electricity, gas, water, and internet) about your move. Arrange for disconnection at your old home and reconnection at the new property.

- Transfer services such as DTH, broadband, and mobile connections to your new address.

B. Address Change Notifications

- Update your address for:
    - Banks, credit cards, insurance, and investment accounts.
    - Employer and government services (Aadhaar, PAN card, vehicle registration).
    - Online shopping accounts (Amazon, Flipkart) and subscriptions.

7. Preparing for Moving Day

A. Final Preparations

- **Moving Company Coordination:** Confirm the moving company's arrival time and provide clear instructions about parking or entry points.

- **Kids and Pets:** Make arrangements for children or pets on moving day to ensure they are safe and out of the way.

- **Inspect the Property:** Do a final walkthrough of your old home to ensure nothing is left behind.

B. On Moving Day

- **Supervise Packing and Loading:** Ensure the movers handle fragile and valuable items carefully.

- **Inventory Check:** Keep a checklist of the items being loaded to cross-check when they are unloaded.

- **Secure Valuables:** Keep important documents, jewelry, and electronics with you instead of handing them over to the movers.

8. Settling into Your New Home

A. Unpacking Strategy

- Start by unpacking the essentials box and setting up the kitchen and bedroom first.

- Unpack room by room, following your labeled boxes.

B. Inspect for Damages

- As you unpack, inspect items for any damage during the move. If you find damages, report them to the moving company immediately.

9. Managing Post-Move Costs

A. Immediate Post-Move Expenses

- Utility deposits, internet setup, minor repairs, or painting in the new home.

- Purchase of new furniture or appliances if needed.

B. Final Settlement with Movers

- Once everything is delivered and unpacked, make the final payment to the moving company and provide feedback or a review.

Summary

Moving in India, whether local or inter-city, requires careful planning and budgeting. By starting early, hiring a reliable moving company, and budgeting for all the necessary expenses, you can make your move efficient and cost-effective. Having a clear plan for packing, organizing, and settling into your new home will minimize stress and ensure a smooth transition.

UTILITIES, ADDRESS CHANGES, AND PREPARING YOUR NEW HOME

When moving to a new home in India, managing utilities, updating your address, and preparing your new home are critical tasks to ensure a smooth transition. Here's a guide to help you organize these aspects efficiently:

1. Managing Utilities in Your New Home

It's essential to transfer or set up utilities in your new home before you move in, so everything is ready when you arrive.

A. Key Utilities to Consider

- **Electricity:** Contact the local electricity board or distribution company (DISCOM) in your area to either transfer the connection or start a new one.
    - How to Transfer: Submit a transfer application to the current provider with ID proof, address proof, and a copy of the sale agreement.
    - New Connection: If it's a new connection, you'll need to apply with documents like an ID proof, proof of ownership, and NOC (No Objection Certificate) from the society or builder.
    - Fees: Costs depend on the region and consumption category but typically range from ₹500 to ₹2,000 for a domestic connection.
- **Water Supply:** Contact your local municipal water supply authority to ensure water services are active. If you're moving into an independent house, you may need to apply for a new connection.
    - Transfer Process: Similar to electricity, an application along with ownership documents, proof of identity, and address proof may be required.
    - Fees: Vary by location and water usage but can range from ₹2,000 to ₹10,000.
- **Piped Gas** (if applicable): Piped natural gas is available in many Indian cities. Contact your regional gas provider to initiate a transfer or new connection.

- ◆ Transfer Process: You'll need to submit an application along with proof of residence, ID proof, and NOC from the society.

- ◆ New Connection: For a new connection, apply online or in person at the gas company's office.

- ◆ Fees: Installation fees are usually between ₹1,500 and ₹3,000, depending on the location.

- **Internet and DTH (Direct-to-Home) TV:** Schedule the disconnection of your old internet and DTH services and arrange for installation in your new home.

  - ◆ How to Transfer: Most service providers allow online transfers through their customer service portal. Alternatively, you can request disconnection and apply for a new connection at the new location.

  - ◆ Fees: Internet installation can range from ₹500 to ₹2,000 depending on the speed and plan. DTH installation fees vary based on the provider, typically around ₹500 to ₹1,500.

2. Address Change Notifications

Updating your address is important to avoid missing out on important mail, bills, or official communications. Here's a checklist of places and services where you should update your address:

A. Financial Institutions

- Banks and Credit Cards: Notify your bank to update your mailing and residential address. This ensures that statements, credit card bills, and other important communications reach you.

  - ◆ Most banks offer an option to update the address through internet banking or by visiting the branch with ID and address proof.

  - ◆ Documents Required: Aadhaar card, passport, or utility bills as address proof.

- Investment Accounts and Insurance: Update your address with investment platforms (like mutual funds, stock brokers) and insurance providers (for health, life, and car insurance).

B. Government Documents

- Aadhaar Card: You can update your Aadhaar card online by visiting the official UIDAI website or by visiting an Aadhaar Enrolment Center.

- PAN Card: While PAN card address updates can't be done directly, you can update your address with the Income Tax Department through an income tax portal profile.

- Voter ID Card: You can update your voter ID online through the National Voter Service Portal (NVSP).

- Passport: If you have moved permanently or plan to stay long-term, update your passport address by submitting a request through the Passport Seva Kendra.

C. Utility and Subscription Services

- Mobile Service Providers: Update your mobile service provider with the new address. This can be done through their respective apps or by visiting a service center with proof of the new address.

- Online Shopping and Delivery Services: Update your address on platforms like Amazon, Flipkart, and grocery delivery apps to avoid deliveries going to your old home.

- Subscriptions: Update the address for any magazine, newspaper, or other regular subscriptions you receive.

D. Employer

- Inform your HR department or employer of your new address to ensure tax filings, employee benefits, and communication are properly updated.

E. Schools and Educational Institutions

- If you have children, inform their schools about the new address for updating their records, sending reports, and emergency contacts.

3. Preparing Your New Home

Before moving in, take some time to prepare your new home for a smooth transition. Here's what you need to focus on:

A. Inspect the Property

- **General Inspection:** Check if all repairs and renovations (if any) have been completed. Look out for issues like leaks, electrical faults, or plumbing problems that need to be fixed before moving in.

- **Pest Control:** It's a good idea to arrange for pest control services before moving in, especially if the house has been unoccupied for some time.

- **Cleaning:** Schedule a deep cleaning of the house, including areas like the kitchen, bathrooms, and hard-to-reach places like under cabinets or behind furniture. Professional cleaning services can handle this if needed.

B. Install Essential Appliances

- **Kitchen Appliances:** Make sure the kitchen is ready with installed appliances such as gas stoves, water purifiers, and refrigerators.

- **Lighting and Fans:** Ensure that all lights and ceiling fans are functional, and replace any bulbs or switches if needed.

- **Water Heaters:** If your new home doesn't already have water heaters, consider installing them in bathrooms for your comfort.

C. Safety and Security

- **Change Locks:** It's wise to change the locks on all external doors to ensure safety. If you're moving into a society or gated community, you can also install digital locks for added security.

- **Install CCTV (if needed):** If you are concerned about security, consider installing CCTV cameras, particularly at entry points.

- **Smoke and Gas Leak Detectors:** Installing these in the kitchen and other critical areas can enhance the safety of your new home.

D. Set Up Furniture

- Plan your furniture placement ahead of time so that movers can place everything correctly upon arrival.

- **Essential Furniture First:** Set up key furniture items like your bed, dining table, and seating arrangements so you can comfortably settle in during the first few days.

E. Internet and TV Setup

- Ensure that your internet and TV services are set up before or soon after the move. This includes installing your router, wiring for DTH, and any additional equipment for smart TVs.

4. Settling in After the Move

Once everything is set up, take the time to make your new house feel like home:

- Unpack Essentials First: Start with essential items like bedding, kitchen utensils, and toiletries.

- Personalize the Space: Hang pictures, place plants, and arrange décor to make your new home feel cozy.

- Greet Neighbours: Introduce yourself to your neighbours, especially if you are new to the area. This will help you feel more integrated into the community.

Summary

Properly managing your utilities, updating your address, and preparing your new home in India ensures a smooth transition to your new living space. Planning ahead, setting up utilities in advance, and organizing the move will help reduce stress and allow you to settle into your new home quickly and comfortably.

CHAPTER 9

LIFE AS HOMEOWNER

Budgeting for Home Maintenance and Repairs

Budgeting for home maintenance and repairs in India is crucial to ensuring your property remains in good condition and avoids major costs from neglect or unexpected damage. Here's how you can create a comprehensive home maintenance and repair budget, along with common expenses you should anticipate:

1. Understanding the Importance of a Home Maintenance Budget

Regular maintenance helps:

- **Preserve Property Value:** Keeping your home in good condition enhances its long-term value.

- **Prevent Costly Repairs:** Routine maintenance can identify small issues before they turn into expensive problems.

- **Ensure Safety:** Timely repair of electrical, plumbing, and structural issues ensures the safety of occupants.

2. Recommended Budget for Home Maintenance

The rule of thumb for home maintenance budgeting is **1% to 3% of the property's value annually**. However, factors like the age of the home, climate, and local costs will influence this amount.

A. Example) Calculation:

- **Property Value:** ₹50,00,000

- **Annual Maintenance Budget:** 1% to 3% = ₹50,000 to ₹1,50,000 annually

For new homes, budgeting 1% may be enough, but older homes, especially those over 10-15 years, may require 2%-3% annually due to increased wear and tear.

3. Categories of Home Maintenance and Repairs

To create a balanced budget, categorize expenses by frequency and type of maintenance needed:

A. Routine Maintenance (Monthly/Quarterly/Annually)

- **Cleaning and General Upkeep:**
  - **Cost:** ₹1,000 - ₹3,000 per month
  - This includes regular cleaning of floors, windows, furniture, and kitchen appliances.
- **Pest Control:**
  - **Cost:** ₹1,000 - ₹3,000 per visit, depending on the size of the home and type of service (quarterly visits recommended).
- **Gardening/Landscaping:**
  - **Cost:** ₹500 - ₹5,000 per month (depends on the size of the garden and region).
- **Servicing Water Purifiers and Air Conditioners:**
  - **Water Purifier:** ₹500 - ₹2,000 annually for filter replacement and maintenance.
  - **Air Conditioner:** ₹500 - ₹1,500 per service, twice a year before summer and after monsoon.

B. Periodic Repairs (Every 2-5 Years)

- **Painting and Wall Repairs:**
  - **Cost:** ₹10,000 - ₹1,00,000 depending on the size of the home, type of paint, and region.
  - External painting may need to be done every 3-5 years due to weather conditions, while internal painting can be done every 4-6 years.
- **Electrical Maintenance:**
  - **Cost:** ₹2,000 - ₹10,000 annually for small repairs, rewiring, or replacing fixtures.
  - This includes checking electrical outlets, switches, and wiring.
- **Plumbing Repairs:**
  - **Cost:** ₹1,000 - ₹10,000 depending on issues (leaky faucets, drain cleaning, pipe replacement).

- ♦ It's important to service or replace water heaters, fix leaks, and ensure proper drainage.

- **Roof Repairs (if applicable):**
  - ♦ **Cost:** ₹5,000 - ₹50,000 depending on the extent of repairs required.
  - ♦ If you live in an independent house, keep a budget for roof maintenance every 5-10 years, especially after monsoons.

C. Major Repairs or Upgrades (5-10 Years)

- **Flooring Replacement or Repairs:**
  - ♦ **Cost:** ₹20,000 - ₹1,00,000 depending on the area and material (tiles, wood, marble, etc.).
  - ♦ Minor repairs or replacements might be necessary over time for wear and tear.

- **Bathroom and Kitchen Renovations:**
  - ♦ **Cost:** ₹50,000 - ₹5,00,000 based on the extent of renovation and choice of materials.
  - ♦ Updating tiles, faucets, cabinets, and appliances every 7-10 years is common.

- **Window and Door Replacement:**
  - ♦ **Cost:** ₹10,000 - ₹50,000 depending on materials (wood, UPVC, Aluminium) and number of windows/doors.
  - ♦ Older homes may require window and door repairs or replacements for better insulation or aesthetics.

D. Seasonal Maintenance

- **Monsoon Preparation:**
  - ♦ **Waterproofing:** ₹10,000 - ₹50,000 depending on the extent of work required to prevent leaks.
  - ♦ **Roof and Gutter Cleaning:** ₹1,000 - ₹5,000 to ensure drainage systems are working.

- **Winter Maintenance (for colder regions):**
  - ♦ **Heater and Insulation Checks:** ₹2,000 - ₹10,000 for heater servicing and insulation upkeep.

4. Prioritizing Maintenance Tasks

It's important to prioritize tasks based on urgency and importance to avoid costly breakdowns.

A. Must-Do Tasks:

- **Safety Issues:** Electrical faults, gas leaks, or structural damage should be fixed immediately to ensure safety.
- **Plumbing Problems:** Leaks, water supply issues, or drainage clogs can lead to bigger problems if ignored.
- **Roof and Waterproofing:** Protect your home from water damage, especially before and after the monsoon season.

B. Low-Priority Tasks:

- **Cosmetic Changes:** Updating wall colours or installing new tiles can be delayed if there are more pressing repair needs.
- **Minor Furniture Repairs:** Unless they affect daily use, these can be scheduled when convenient.

5. Emergency Repair Fund

In addition to the annual maintenance budget, it's a good idea to set aside an **emergency fund** for unexpected repairs such as:

- **Burst Pipes or Major Leaks**
- **Electrical Failures**
- **Appliance Breakdown (refrigerator, washing machine, etc.)**

Recommended Emergency Fund: ₹10,000 - ₹50,000, depending on the size of your home and the age of the structure.

6. Hiring Professional Help vs DIY

A. Hiring Professionals:

- For major repairs or technical tasks (electrical, plumbing, structural work), it's safer and more efficient to hire licensed professionals.
- **Average Costs:**
    - Electricians: ₹300 - ₹1,000 per visit

- ◆ Plumbers: ₹200 - ₹800 per visit
- ◆ Carpenters: ₹500 - ₹2,000 for small repairs

B. DIY for Small Repairs:

- For minor tasks like changing light bulbs, tightening loose screws, or painting a small area, you can save money by doing it yourself.

- **Tools to Invest In:** Basic tools like a screwdriver set, hammer, tape measure, and pliers.

7. Monitoring and Updating Your Budget

It's important to keep track of your actual expenses against your budget. This allows you to adjust future budgets based on your home's specific maintenance needs.

- **Track Costs:** Use a spreadsheet or a home maintenance app to track spending.

- **Annual Review:** Review your budget annually and adjust it based on the age of your home, inflation, and any major repairs needed.

Summary

Home maintenance and repair budgeting in India is essential for ensuring the longevity and safety of your property. By setting aside 1%-3% of your home's value annually, creating a prioritized plan for routine, periodic, and emergency tasks, and keeping an emergency fund, you can avoid surprise expenses and keep your home in optimal condition.

BUILDING EQUITY AND UNDERSTANDING HOME VALUE

Building equity and understanding home value are essential concepts for homeownership in India, particularly for first-time buyers. Equity represents your ownership stake in the property, while the home's value can fluctuate over time, affecting your overall investment. Here's a detailed breakdown to help you grasp these concepts in the Indian context:

1. What is Equity?

Equity is the portion of the home that you truly own, calculated as the difference between the home's current market value and the outstanding mortgage balance.

A. Formula for Calculating Home Equity:

- **Home Equity = Current Market Value of the Home – Outstanding Loan Balance**

For example, if your home's market value is ₹75,00,000 and you still owe ₹35,00,000 on your home loan, your equity would be:

- **₹75,00,000 - ₹35,00,000 = ₹40,00,000**

This ₹40,00,000 is your equity in the home, which grows as you repay the mortgage or as the value of the home appreciates.

2. Why is Building Equity Important?

Equity serves multiple purposes in homeownership:

- **Wealth Creation:** As you build equity, you increase your net worth since the home becomes a valuable financial asset.

- **Collateral for Loans:** You can use your home's equity as collateral to take out loans (home equity loans or lines of credit), which may be useful for renovations, education, or emergencies.

- **Selling for a Profit:** When you sell your home, the more equity you have, the higher the profit potential after paying off the remaining loan balance.

3. How to Build Equity in Your Home

There are several ways to increase your equity over time:

A. Pay Down Your Loan

- **Regular EMI Payments:** As you pay your monthly EMIs (equated monthly instalments), your loan principal reduces over time, increasing your equity.

- **Making Additional Payments:** If you have surplus funds, you can make additional payments toward the principal to reduce the loan balance faster, thus building equity more quickly.

B. Home Value Appreciation

- **Property Market Growth:** Over time, property values tend to rise due to factors like urbanization, infrastructure development, and demand for housing.

  - Example: A home bought for ₹50,00,000 could be worth ₹70,00,000 after 10 years, which increases your equity.

- **Improvements and Renovations:** Making strategic improvements like modernizing the kitchen, renovating bathrooms, or adding amenities like solar panels can increase the market value of your home.

C. Increase Your Down Payment

- **Higher Down Payment:** When purchasing a home, a larger down payment means you own a bigger portion of the home right from the start, giving you higher equity at the outset.

  - In India, lenders typically require a down payment of 20% of the home's value. Increasing this percentage can give you more equity early on.

4. Understanding Home Value in India

The value of a home is influenced by multiple factors, and understanding these can help you make informed decisions whether you're buying, selling, or refinancing.

A. Factors That Affect Home Value

- **Location:** Proximity to schools, hospitals, public transport, shopping centers, and employment hubs significantly impacts the property's value.

- **Local Infrastructure and Development:** Upcoming infrastructure projects like metro lines, highways, or airports can boost property values in the surrounding areas.

- **Economic Conditions:** Overall economic health, interest rates, and inflation affect the real estate market. A thriving economy usually leads to property appreciation, while a downturn may cause prices to stagnate or fall.

- **Demand and Supply:** If demand for homes in a specific area exceeds supply, prices will rise. Conversely, a market with too many homes available may see stagnant or falling prices.

- **Age and Condition of the Property:** Newer homes or well-maintained older homes typically command higher prices. Neglected properties or those requiring significant repairs might see lower valuations.

- **Legal Status and Documentation:** Homes with clear titles, proper approvals, and compliance with local regulations are valued higher than properties with legal issues or incomplete documentation.

B. How to Assess Home Value

- **Comparable Sales (Market Approach):** Look at recent sales of similar homes in the same area (size, age, amenities) to estimate the value of your home.

- **Government Circle Rates:** The circle rate is the minimum rate at which a property can be sold, as determined by the state government. While not reflective of the true market price, it provides a baseline for valuation.

- **Online Valuation Tools:** Real estate platforms like Magicbricks, 99acres, and Housing.com provide tools to estimate property values based on location and property type.

- **Professional Valuation:** Hiring a certified property valuer can give you an accurate assessment of your home's worth, considering market trends, property condition, and other factors.

C. Property Appreciation Rates in India

- On average, properties in major cities like Mumbai, Delhi, Bengaluru, and Pune appreciate by 5%-10% annually, though rates can vary based on location and market conditions.

- For example, real estate in upcoming metro cities like Hyderabad and Ahmedabad may see faster appreciation due to rising demand and growing infrastructure, while Tier 2 and Tier 3 cities may have slower growth rates.

5. Leveraging Equity for Future Investments

As you build equity, you can tap into it for further financial goals, such as:

- **Home Equity Loans:** You can borrow against the equity in your home to fund large expenses like renovations, education, or business investments. These loans are generally easier to get and offer lower interest rates compared to unsecured loans.

- **Refinancing Your Home Loan:** If the value of your home has significantly increased, you can refinance your mortgage to access better loan terms or withdraw some of the equity for other purposes.

- **Upgrading to a New Home:** If your home's value has appreciated substantially, you may decide to sell and use the profits (your equity) to buy a larger or more valuable property.

6. Risks to Home Equity and Value

While building equity and understanding home value are important, it's crucial to be aware of potential risks:

- **Falling Property Prices:** If property values decline due to economic downturns or oversupply in the area, your equity could shrink, especially if the market value drops below your loan balance.

- **Over-leveraging:** Taking out too many home equity loans or refinancing without a clear repayment strategy can lead to debt problems.

- **Neglecting Maintenance:** Poor home maintenance can reduce the property's value over time, lowering your equity and making it harder to sell the home at a good price.

7. Tips to Maximize Equity and Home Value in India

- **Regular Maintenance:** Invest in small, regular maintenance to prevent larger problems that could reduce your home's value.

- **Strategic Renovations:** Focus on high-value areas like kitchens and bathrooms, which tend to increase resale value.

- **Stay Informed about Market Trends:** Track property prices and market developments in your area to decide the best time to sell, refinance, or make improvements.

- **Ensure Proper Documentation:** Maintain clear legal titles and all necessary approvals to ensure your home retains its value in case of sale or refinancing.

Summary

Building equity and understanding home value are key components of long-term wealth creation through homeownership in India. By making smart financial decisions, regularly maintaining your property, and staying informed about market trends, you can maximize the value of your home and the equity you build over time.

INSURANCE AND PROPERTY TAXES: WHAT YOU NEED TO KNOW

When purchasing a home in India, understanding **insurance** and **property taxes** is crucial. Both aspects are essential for safeguarding your investment and ensuring you remain compliant with legal obligations. Here's a detailed guide to help you understand what you need to know about home insurance and property taxes in India.

1. Home Insurance in India

Home insurance provides financial protection against damages or losses caused by unforeseen events like natural disasters, fires, theft, or accidents. While not mandatory, it is highly recommended to protect your home, one of your most valuable assets.

A. Types of Home Insurance in India

There are various types of home insurance policies available in India, tailored to cover different aspects of your home:

- **Standard Fire and Special Perils Policy:**
  - **Covers:** Damages caused by fire, lightning, storm, flood, earthquake, and explosion.
  - **Example:** If your house is damaged due to an earthquake or flood, this policy will help cover the cost of repairs.
- **Home Structure Insurance:**
  - **Covers:** The structure of your home, including walls, roofs, and fixtures, against physical damage from natural calamities.
  - **Example:** If a storm causes a part of your roof to collapse, this insurance will cover the repair costs.
- **Home Contents Insurance:**
  - **Covers:** The contents inside your home, such as furniture, electronics, appliances, jewellery, and other personal belongings.
  - **Example:** If your home is burglarized and valuable items are stolen, the policy will compensate for the loss.
- **Comprehensive Home Insurance:**
  - **Covers:** Both the structure and the contents of the home.

♦ **Example:** If a fire damages both the house and the contents, this policy will provide coverage for both.

B. Factors Affecting Home Insurance Premiums

- **Location:** Homes in flood-prone or earthquake-prone areas may have higher premiums.
- **Home Value and Size:** Larger homes and more expensive properties attract higher premiums.
- **Construction Material:** Homes made with fire-resistant materials may have lower premiums.
- **Age of the Home:** Newer homes often have lower premiums due to reduced risk of structural issues.

C. Key Features to Look for in a Policy

- **Sum Insured:** Ensure that the sum insured adequately covers the replacement cost of the structure and contents.
- **Add-on Coverage:** You can opt for add-ons such as burglary cover, terrorism cover, or coverage for temporary accommodation if the home becomes uninhabitable.
- **Claim Settlement Ratio:** Check the insurer's claim settlement ratio, which reflects their efficiency in settling claims.

D. Popular Home Insurance Providers in India

- **ICICI Lombard**
- **HDFC Ergo**
- **Bajaj Allianz**
- **Tata AIG**

2. Property Taxes in India

Property tax is a recurring expense that every homeowner must pay to the local municipal corporation or local body. The tax revenue is used by local authorities to provide civic services such as maintenance of roads, parks, street lighting, and sewage systems.

A. What is Property Tax?

Property tax is levied on the real estate you own, and it is based on the location, size, and usage of the property (residential, commercial, or industrial).

B. How is Property Tax Calculated?

The method of calculation may vary depending on the state or municipal body, but the most common methods used in India are:

- **Annual Rental Value System (ARV):**
  - ◆ **Basis:** The tax is calculated based on the rental income that the property can generate in a year, irrespective of whether the property is rented or self-occupied.
  - ◆ **Used In:** Cities like Chennai.
- **Capital Value System (CVS):**
  - ◆ **Basis:** The tax is based on a percentage of the market value of the property, determined by the local government.
  - ◆ **Used In:** Cities like Mumbai.
- **Unit Area Value System (UAV):**
  - ◆ **Basis:** Tax is levied based on the per-unit price of the built-up area or carpet area of the property. This rate is set by the municipal body and depends on the location and usage.
  - ◆ **Used In:** Delhi, Bengaluru, and Kolkata.

C. Factors Influencing Property Tax

- **Location of the Property:** Properties in prime urban locations attract higher taxes.
- **Size of the Property:** Larger properties or properties with more built-up area incur higher taxes.
- **Property Type:** Commercial properties are taxed at higher rates compared to residential ones.
- **Property Age:** Older properties may have a lower tax rate due to depreciation.
- **Amenities and Infrastructure:** Properties in areas with better infrastructure (parks, schools, roads) may face higher taxes.

D. How to Pay Property Tax

Most municipal bodies in India now allow property tax payments online through their official websites. The process generally involves:

1. **Visit the Official Website** of your city's municipal corporation (e.g., BBMP for Bengaluru, MCGM for Mumbai).

2. **Enter Property Details**, such as your property ID, zone, ward, or address.

3. **Check the Outstanding Amount**, which will be calculated based on the formula set by the local authority.

4. **Pay Online** using net banking, credit/debit cards, or UPI.

You can also visit your local municipal office and pay the tax manually.

E. Consequences of Non-Payment

Failure to pay property tax can lead to:

- **Penalties:** Interest on overdue amounts and fines.

- **Legal Action:** In extreme cases, the municipal body may seize or auction the property to recover the dues.

3. How Home Insurance and Property Taxes Affect You

A. Home Insurance: Financial Protection

- Without home insurance, you are at risk of significant financial loss if your home is damaged by natural disasters, accidents, or theft.

- Having comprehensive insurance helps you avoid unexpected expenses and gives you peace of mind that your property and possessions are protected.

B. Property Taxes: Legal Obligation

- Paying property taxes is a legal requirement, and non-payment can lead to penalties or loss of property. Staying on top of your property tax obligations ensures that you avoid these consequences and remain in good standing with local authorities.

- The amount you pay also indirectly contributes to the upkeep of public services in your area.

4. Tips for Managing Insurance and Property Taxes

- **Review Home Insurance Annually:** Reassess your home insurance policy each year to ensure it provides adequate coverage. Update it if the value of your home increases due to renovations or if you acquire expensive assets.

- **Set Up Property Tax Reminders:** Property taxes are typically paid annually or semi-annually. Mark these dates on your calendar or use online reminders to avoid missing the due date.

- **Consider Tax Exemptions:** Some states offer exemptions or rebates on property taxes for senior citizens, people with disabilities, or properties in certain zones. Check if you qualify for any benefits.

Summary

Understanding **home insurance** and **property taxes** in India is essential for homeowners. While insurance protects your property from unforeseen risks, property taxes are a mandatory obligation that helps maintain local infrastructure. By staying informed and managing these aspects effectively, you can safeguard your home and stay compliant with legal requirements.

TIPS FOR BECOMING A CONFIDENT AND SUCCESSFUL HOMEOWNER

Becoming a confident and successful homeowner in India requires a combination of financial preparation, strategic planning, and a good understanding of property maintenance and management. Here are some key tips to help you navigate homeownership confidently and maximize your experience as a homeowner:

1. Financial Preparedness: Lay a Strong Foundation

A. Create a Budget and Stick to It

- **Before Buying:** Assess your financial health by creating a budget that accounts for your monthly expenses, debts, and income. Ensure that you can afford homeownership without compromising other financial goals.

- **After Buying:** Plan for recurring homeownership expenses like EMIs, property taxes, insurance, maintenance, and utility bills. Allocate a portion of your monthly income to cover these costs comfortably.

B. Build an Emergency Fund

- Unexpected repairs or job loss can happen, so it's important to have at least 6 months of living expenses saved up. This safety net will prevent financial strain during emergencies.

C. Get Pre-Approved for a Loan

- Being pre-approved for a mortgage gives you a clear understanding of how much home you can afford and strengthens your bargaining power when negotiating with sellers.

2. Know Your Rights and Responsibilities as a Homeowner

A. Understand the Legal Aspects

- Familiarize yourself with property-related laws and regulations, such as **RERA (Real Estate Regulation and Development Act)** and local building bylaws. This ensures transparency and helps you avoid legal pitfalls.

- **Title Deeds, Encumbrance Certificates, and Sale Agreements** should be thoroughly verified with the help of a legal expert.

B. Be Aware of Property Taxes and Utility Bills

- Stay up to date with property tax payments to avoid penalties. Also, ensure timely payment of water, electricity, and other utility bills to maintain services uninterrupted.

3. Maintenance and Upkeep: Protect Your Investment

A. Conduct Regular Maintenance

- **Routine Inspections:** Check for plumbing leaks, electrical faults, and roof integrity annually. Routine upkeep prevents bigger, costlier repairs down the line.

- **Preventive Maintenance:** Regularly service appliances like air conditioners, water heaters, and elevators (if applicable). Paint your home every few years to maintain its appearance and prevent structural damage.

B. Create a Maintenance Fund

- Set aside funds monthly for home maintenance and repairs. This fund will help you cover unexpected expenses like fixing water leaks, electrical faults, or replacing old appliances.

4. Improve Energy Efficiency and Sustainability

A. Invest in Energy-Efficient Appliances

- Use energy-efficient lighting (like LED bulbs), install solar panels if feasible, and opt for appliances with high energy star ratings to reduce electricity consumption and save on utility bills.

B. Water Conservation

- Install low-flow faucets, water-efficient toilets, and rainwater harvesting systems. Water is a precious resource in many parts of India, and these changes will also help reduce your water bill.

5. Build Equity and Long-Term Value

A. Make Smart Renovations

- Invest in renovations that add value to your home, such as modernizing the kitchen, upgrading bathrooms, or improving curb appeal. These upgrades can increase your home's resale value.

B. Pay Extra on Your Mortgage

- If possible, make extra payments toward your home loan principal. This reduces the loan tenure and helps you build equity faster.

6. Build a Good Relationship with Your Neighbours

A. Foster Positive Relationships

- A good rapport with your neighbours can enhance your living experience. Neighbours can help in times of emergencies, share local knowledge, and foster a sense of community.

B. Be Involved in the Community

- Attend housing society meetings and stay engaged with local issues. This involvement gives you a say in decisions related to maintenance, security, and amenities in your area.

7. Keep Up with Market Trends

A. Stay Informed about Property Values

- Keep track of market trends in your area to understand how the value of your property is likely to change. This knowledge is crucial if you plan to sell, rent, or refinance your home.

B. Consider Long-Term Appreciation

- If you're planning to stay long-term, consider the appreciation potential of your property. Proximity to upcoming infrastructure, transport hubs, or business centers can significantly increase the future value of your home.

8. Secure Your Home

A. Invest in Security Systems

- Install CCTV cameras, burglar alarms, and smart locks for enhanced security. Gated communities and housing societies often have their own security measures, but it's still wise to secure your individual home.

B. Get Adequate Home Insurance

- Purchase comprehensive home insurance that covers both the structure and the contents. This ensures you're financially protected in case of natural disasters, fire, theft, or accidents.

9. Plan for the Long Term

A. Plan for Future Expenses

- Be prepared for future expenses like major home repairs, appliance replacements, or potential renovations. Consider factors like aging infrastructure or family needs (e.g., expanding the house or adding a room).

B. Think About Future Resale

- Even if you plan to stay in the home for the long term, keep its future resale value in mind. Regular maintenance, smart upgrades, and keeping documentation organized will ensure your home retains its value.

10. Enjoy the Journey of Homeownership

A. Personalize Your Home

- Take the time to personalize your space with furniture, decor, and color schemes that make it feel like home. This boosts emotional satisfaction and comfort in your living space.

B. Celebrate Your Achievements

- Owning a home is a significant milestone, especially in a country like India where real estate is a valuable asset. Take pride in your accomplishment, and remember to celebrate key moments, whether it's moving in or completing renovations.

Summary

Becoming a confident and successful homeowner in India involves financial preparedness, understanding legalities, regular maintenance, and long-term planning. By following these tips, you can make the most of your homeownership experience, increase the value of your investment, and create a secure, comfortable environment for you and your family.

Congratulations on Becoming a Homeowner!

Reflecting on Your Home Buying Journey

Reflecting on your home-buying journey in India can be a valuable exercise to assess your experiences, learn from them, and plan for future improvements or investments. Here's a structured approach to reflecting on this journey:

1. Review Your Initial Goals and Expectations

A. Define Your Objectives

- **Original Goals:** What were your primary goals when you started the home-buying process? (e.g., finding a family home, investment property, or a vacation home)

- **Expectations:** How did your expectations about the buying process, costs, and timelines align with reality?

B. Successes and Challenges

- **Successes:** What aspects of your journey went well? Did you find a home that met your criteria and budget?

- **Challenges:** What were the major challenges you faced? Did you encounter issues with financing, property searches, or legal documentation?

2. Analyze the Financial Aspects

A. Budget Management

- **Initial Budget:** Did you stick to your initial budget? If not, what adjustments did you have to make?

- **Unexpected Costs:** Were there any unexpected costs during the buying process? How did you handle them?

B. Mortgage and Financing

- **Loan Approval:** Was the mortgage approval process smooth? Did you face any hurdles in getting pre-approval or finalizing your loan?

- **Interest Rates:** How did you fare with the interest rates? Did you choose fixed or variable rates, and were you satisfied with the decision?

3. Evaluate the Home Selection Process

A. Property Search

- **Searching Methods:** How effective were the methods you used for searching for properties (online platforms, real estate agents, etc.)?

- **Property Visits:** Did the properties you visited meet your expectations? Were there any discrepancies between online listings and actual properties?

B. Decision-Making

- **Final Choice:** Why did you choose the particular property? What factors influenced your decision the most?

- **Negotiations:** How was the negotiation process? Were you able to secure a good deal, or did you face difficulties?

4. Reflect on Legal and Documentation Aspects

A. Legalities

- **Documentation:** Was the documentation process clear and straightforward? Did you encounter any issues with property titles, agreements, or approvals?

- **Legal Assistance:** Did you engage a legal expert? If so, how helpful were they in ensuring that all legal aspects were covered?

B. Closing Process

- **Closing Day:** Was the closing process as expected? Did you face any last-minute issues or surprises?

- **Understanding Costs:** Were you fully aware of all closing costs and fees involved? How did they impact your overall budget?

5. Assess Your Experience with Homeownership

A. Settling In

- **Move-In Experience:** How was your experience moving into your new home? Were there any challenges or surprises?

- **Home Setup:** Did you face any difficulties setting up utilities, changing addresses, or getting settled in?

B. Maintenance and Upkeep

- **Maintenance Issues:** Have you encountered any maintenance or repair issues since moving in? How have you managed them?

- **Home Improvements:** Have you made any improvements or renovations? How did these impact your satisfaction with the home?

6. Evaluate Your Overall Satisfaction

A. Personal Satisfaction

- **Living Experience:** Are you happy with your decision to buy this home? Does it meet your needs and lifestyle?

- **Investment Value:** How do you feel about the value of your investment? Are you seeing the appreciation or benefits you anticipated?

B. Lessons Learned

- **Positive Takeaways:** What lessons have you learned from this experience that you would carry forward to future real estate decisions?

- **Areas for Improvement:** Are there any areas where you feel you could have made better decisions or approached things differently?

7. Plan for the Future

A. Long-Term Goals

- **Future Plans:** What are your long-term plans for this property? Are you considering any future renovations, upgrades, or even moving to a new home?

- **Investment Strategy:** If this property was purchased as an investment, how do you plan to manage or leverage it moving forward?

B. Continuing Education

- **Stay Informed:** Keep yourself updated on real estate trends, market changes, and legal updates to make informed decisions in the future.

Summary

Reflecting on your home-buying journey allows you to evaluate your experiences, understand what worked well, and identify areas for improvement. This process not only helps you gain insights but also prepares you for future real estate ventures, whether you're looking to buy another property or make changes to your current one.

FUTURE CONSIDERATIONS: REFINANCING, SELLING AND INVESTING IN REAL ESTATE

When contemplating future considerations such as refinancing, selling, or investing in real estate in India, it's important to have a strategic approach. Each decision impacts your financial situation and long-term goals. Here's a comprehensive guide to help you navigate these aspects:

1. Refinancing Your Mortgage

A. Understanding Refinancing

Refinancing involves replacing your current mortgage with a new one, typically with better terms. This can be beneficial if interest rates have dropped, or if you want to alter the loan term or switch from a variable to a fixed rate.

B. When to Consider Refinancing

- **Interest Rates:** If current interest rates are significantly lower than when you initially took out your loan, refinancing can reduce your monthly payments and overall interest cost.

- **Loan Terms:** If you want to change the loan term (e.g., from a 30-year to a 15-year mortgage) to pay off the loan faster or to reduce monthly payments, refinancing can help.

- **Equity Build-Up:** If you've built significant equity in your home, refinancing can allow you to access some of this equity for other purposes like home improvements or debt consolidation.

C. Steps to Refinance

- **Assess Your Financial Goals:** Determine why you want to refinance and what you hope to achieve.

- **Compare Lenders:** Shop around for the best rates and terms from various lenders. Consider both banks and non-banking financial companies (NBFCs).

- **Calculate Costs:** Evaluate the costs associated with refinancing, such as processing fees, prepayment penalties, and legal charges.

- **Apply for Refinancing:** Submit your application, including required documents like proof of income, credit history, and property details.

- **Complete the Process:** If approved, finalize the new mortgage and pay off the old loan.

D. Pros and Cons of Refinancing

- **Pros:** Lower monthly payments, reduced interest rate, potential access to home equity.

- **Cons:** Closing costs, potential extension of loan term, or fees for early loan repayment.

2. Selling Your Property

A. Preparing to Sell

- **Evaluate Property Value:** Get a professional appraisal or comparative market analysis (CMA) to understand your property's current market value.

- **Enhance Curb Appeal:** Make necessary repairs and improvements to increase the property's attractiveness. Consider staging your home to appeal to potential buyers.

- **Hire a Real Estate Agent:** Choose a reputable real estate agent who understands the local market and can help with pricing, marketing, and negotiations.

B. Selling Process

- **Set the Price:** Based on the appraisal and market conditions, set a competitive price.

- **Market the Property:** Use various channels such as online listings, social media, and real estate networks to reach potential buyers.

- **Negotiate Offers:** Review offers, negotiate terms, and accept the most favorable offer.

- **Complete the Sale:** Finalize the sale by completing legal documentation, transferring ownership, and settling any outstanding costs.

C. Tax Implications

- **Capital Gains Tax:** Be aware of capital gains tax implications if the property value has increased significantly. In India, short-term capital gains are taxed as per your income tax slab, while long-term gains are taxed at 20% with indexation benefits.

3. Investing in Real Estate

A. Types of Real Estate Investments

- **Residential Properties:** Investing in apartments, villas, or houses for rental income or future appreciation.

- **Commercial Properties:** Offices, retail spaces, or industrial properties that can provide higher rental yields but require more capital and involve higher risk.

- **Land:** Buying undeveloped land for future development or resale. Land investment can offer significant appreciation if located in a growing area.

B. Factors to Consider

- **Location:** Choose locations with high growth potential, good infrastructure, and demand for rental properties. Research upcoming infrastructure projects or business developments.

- **Market Trends:** Stay updated on real estate market trends, property prices, and economic factors that could influence the investment's performance.

- **Rental Yield:** Calculate the expected rental income versus the property's cost to assess potential returns.

- **Legal Compliance:** Ensure all legal aspects are covered, including property titles, zoning regulations, and compliance with RERA.

C. Financing Your Investment

- **Loans:** Consider financing options such as home loans, personal loans, or commercial property loans. Evaluate interest rates, loan terms, and eligibility criteria.

- **Investment Partners:** You can also explore joint ventures or partnerships to share the financial burden and risks.

D. Managing Your Investment

- **Property Management:** If renting out, decide whether to manage the property yourself or hire a property management company.

- **Maintenance:** Regularly maintain the property to ensure it remains attractive to tenants and retains its value.

E. Exit Strategy

- **Plan Ahead:** Have an exit strategy in place, whether it's selling the property, refinancing, or holding it for long-term appreciation.
- **Market Timing:** Monitor market conditions to time your exit strategically for the best returns.

4. Future Planning and Considerations

A. Personal and Financial Goals

- Align your real estate decisions with your long-term personal and financial goals. Consider how buying, selling, or investing fits into your overall life plan.

B. Market Research

- Continuously research market trends, economic conditions, and policy changes that could impact real estate investments and property values.

C. Professional Advice

- Seek advice from real estate professionals, financial advisors, and legal experts to make informed decisions and optimize your real estate strategies.

Summary

Strategically managing future considerations such as refinancing, selling, or investing in real estate in India requires careful planning, research, and professional guidance. By understanding the processes and potential impacts of each decision, you can navigate these aspects effectively and make choices that align with your financial goals and aspirations.

ADDITIONAL RESOURCES AND NEXT STEPS

Here's a guide to additional resources and next steps to help you navigate the real estate landscape in India effectively:

1. Additional Resources

A. Government Websites and Portals

- **RERA (Real Estate Regulation and Development Act) Portal:** Provides information on property regulations, developer registration, and consumer grievances. RERA Portal

- **Housing and Urban Affairs Ministry:** Offers insights into housing schemes, policies, and urban development. Ministry of Housing and Urban Affairs

- **Income Tax Department:** For information on tax implications related to real estate transactions. Income Tax India

B. Real Estate Associations

- **CREDAI (Confederation of Real Estate Developers' Associations of India):** Provides updates on real estate trends, market reports, and developer standards. CREDAI

- **NAR-India (National Association of Realtors - India):** Offers resources for real estate professionals and investors. NAR-India

C. Financial and Investment Platforms

- **Mutual Fund Platforms:** Websites like Groww and Zerodha for investment advice and financial planning.

- **Real Estate Investment Platforms:** Explore platforms like PropTiger and Housing.com for property listings and market analysis.

D. Legal and Compliance

- **Legal Consultants:** Platforms like LawRato and LegalDesk offer legal advice and documentation services.

- **Property Title Search Services:** Use services like VerifyMyProperty for title verification and legal checks.

E. Real Estate Market Reports

- **Research Reports:** Look for reports from real estate research firms like <u>JLL India</u> and <u>CBRE India</u> for market insights and trends.

F. Online Forums and Communities

- **Real Estate Forums:** Join forums like <u>IndiaPropertyForum</u> and <u>UrbanClap</u> for discussions and advice from other real estate professionals and investors.

2. Next Steps

A. Define Your Goals

- **Short-Term Goals:** Identify immediate needs, such as refinancing, buying, or selling a property.
- **Long-Term Goals:** Set long-term objectives for your real estate investments, including retirement planning or wealth building.

B. Conduct Market Research

- **Local Market Trends:** Research the real estate market in your desired location. Analyze property prices, rental yields, and market demand.
- **Economic Indicators:** Keep an eye on economic indicators that affect real estate, such as interest rates, inflation, and employment rates.

C. Consult Professionals

- **Real Estate Agent:** Engage a reputable real estate agent for buying, selling, or renting properties.
- **Financial Advisor:** Consult a financial advisor to understand the financial implications of real estate transactions and investment strategies.
- **Legal Expert:** Seek legal advice for property documentation, title verification, and compliance with local regulations.

D. Review and Update Financial Plans

- **Budget Review:** Regularly review your budget and financial plans to accommodate changes in income, expenses, and investment goals.

- **Loan Options:** Evaluate and compare loan options if considering refinancing or taking a new mortgage.

E. Explore Investment Opportunities

- **Property Investment:** Explore different types of real estate investments, such as residential, commercial, or land.

- **Diversification:** Consider diversifying your investment portfolio to include other asset classes, such as stocks, bonds, or mutual funds.

F. Stay Informed

- **Market Updates:** Subscribe to real estate newsletters and market reports to stay updated on trends and opportunities.

- **Regulatory Changes:** Keep track of changes in real estate regulations and policies that may impact your investments or transactions.

G. Plan for Maintenance and Management

- **Property Management:** If you own rental properties, decide whether to manage them yourself or hire a property management company.

- **Maintenance Schedule:** Create a maintenance schedule to keep your property in good condition and address any issues promptly.

H. Build a Network

- **Industry Connections:** Network with other real estate professionals, investors, and industry experts to gain insights and opportunities.

- **Community Engagement:** Participate in local real estate forums, seminars, and workshops to enhance your knowledge and stay connected with the industry.

Summary

Navigating the real estate landscape in India requires a combination of research, professional advice, and strategic planning. By utilizing these resources and taking the outlined next steps, you can make informed decisions, manage your investments effectively, and achieve your real estate goals.

GLOSSARY OF REAL ESTATE TERMS IN INDIA

Here's a comprehensive glossary of common real estate terms in India to help you navigate the property market effectively:

A

Agreement to Sale: A legal document that outlines the terms and conditions agreed upon between the buyer and seller before the final sale deed is executed.

Amortization: The process of gradually repaying a loan through regular payments of principal and interest over a specified period.

Asset: Any property or item of value owned by an individual or entity, including real estate.

B

Broker: A professional who facilitates the buying, selling, or renting of properties, typically earning a commission for their services.

Builder: A person or company engaged in the construction of residential or commercial properties.

Builder Floor: A type of residential property where an entire floor of a building is sold as an independent unit.

Buyer's Agent: A real estate agent who represents the interests of the buyer in a property transaction.

C

Capital Gains: The profit realized from the sale of an asset, such as property, that has increased in value over time.

Carpet Area: The actual usable area within the walls of an apartment or property, excluding common areas like corridors and staircases.

Clause: A specific provision or condition in a legal document or agreement.

Completion Certificate: A document issued by the local municipal authority confirming that a construction project complies with all regulations and is ready for occupancy.

Condition Precedent: A condition that must be fulfilled before a contract becomes legally binding.

D

Deed: A legal document that transfers ownership of property from one party to another.

Deposit: An amount of money paid upfront to secure a property or as a down payment towards its purchase.

Developer: A company or individual responsible for developing, constructing, and sometimes marketing real estate projects.

Draft Agreement: A preliminary version of a legal agreement or contract that outlines the terms before the final version is executed.

E

Encumbrance Certificate: A document that certifies that a property is free from any legal liabilities or claims.

Equity: The difference between the market value of a property and the amount owed on the mortgage or loan.

Escrow: A financial arrangement where a third party holds and manages funds or documents until certain conditions are met.

F

Fixed Rate Mortgage: A mortgage with an interest rate that remains constant throughout the term of the loan.

Foreclosure: The legal process by which a lender takes possession of a property due to the borrower's failure to repay the mortgage.

G

Grandfather Clause: A provision in a contract or regulation that allows an existing situation to continue even if new regulations are introduced.

Gated Community: A residential area with controlled access and security measures, often offering additional amenities like parks and clubhouses.

H

Home Loan: A loan provided by financial institutions to purchase or build a residential property, typically with regular repayments over a specified period.

Holding Period: The length of time an investor holds a property before selling it.

I

Interest Rate: The percentage of the loan amount charged by the lender as interest on the borrowed sum.

Investment Property: Real estate purchased with the intention of earning rental income or capital appreciation.

Indexation: The adjustment of the property's cost to account for inflation, affecting the calculation of capital gains tax.

J

Joint Ownership: Ownership of property by two or more individuals, where each has a legal interest in the property.

Joint Venture: A business arrangement where two or more parties collaborate to invest in and develop a real estate project.

L

Land Title: The legal right to own, use, or transfer a piece of land, as evidenced by a land title document.

Lease: A legal agreement that grants a tenant the right to use a property for a specified period in exchange for rent.

Lien: A legal claim or right against property used as security for a debt or obligation.

Loan-to-Value Ratio (LTV): The ratio of the loan amount to the appraised value of the property, used by lenders to assess risk.

M

Mortgage: A loan taken out to purchase or refinance a property, where the property itself serves as collateral.

Mortgage Insurance: Insurance that protects the lender in case the borrower defaults on the mortgage.

Market Value: The estimated price a property would sell for in the open market, based on recent comparable sales and market conditions.

N

No Objection Certificate (NOC): A document issued by authorities or parties involved, stating that they have no objection to a specific transaction or action.

Notarized Document: A legal document that has been certified by a notary public, verifying the authenticity of signatures and contents.

O

Offer to Purchase: A formal proposal made by a buyer to purchase a property, outlining the price and terms.

Occupancy Certificate: A certificate issued by local authorities confirming that a property is suitable for occupation as per regulations.

P

Pre-approval: The process of getting preliminary approval for a mortgage loan based on a buyer's financial status and creditworthiness.

Property Management: The administration and maintenance of real estate properties, typically handled by a property management company or individual.

Possession: The act of taking physical control and ownership of a property, usually after the final sale and completion of legal formalities.

Power of Attorney (POA): A legal document authorizing one person to act on behalf of another in property transactions or legal matters.

R

Real Estate Investment Trust (REIT): A company that owns, operates, or finances income-producing real estate and offers shares to investors.

Rent Agreement: A legal contract between a landlord and tenant outlining the terms and conditions of renting a property.

Registration: The legal process of recording a property transaction with the relevant authority to make it legally binding.

RERA (Real Estate Regulation and Development Act): An Indian law designed to regulate and promote transparency in the real estate sector, ensuring protection for buyers and developers.

S

Sale Deed: A legal document that formally transfers ownership of a property from the seller to the buyer.

Stamp Duty: A tax levied by the government on the legal documents related to the transfer of property ownership.

Sub-Lease: A lease agreement where the original tenant rents out the property to another tenant.

Settlement: The process of resolving the financial and legal aspects of a property transaction, including payment and transfer of ownership.

T

Title Deed: A legal document that proves ownership of a property.

Tenancy: The arrangement where a tenant is granted the right to occupy and use a property for a specified period in exchange for rent.

Transfer of Property: The legal process of transferring ownership rights from one party to another.

U

Under Construction: A property that is currently being built and is not yet completed or ready for occupancy.

Usage Rights: The rights granted to a property owner or tenant to use the property for specified purposes.

V

Valuation: The process of determining the market value of a property based on factors like location, condition, and comparable sales.

Variable Rate Mortgage: A mortgage with an interest rate that can change periodically based on market conditions.

W

Will: A legal document that specifies how a person's property and assets should be distributed upon their death.

Warranty: A guarantee provided by the seller or developer regarding the condition and quality of the property.

X

Xclusive Right: A legal term referring to exclusive rights granted to an individual or entity over a property, such as the right to sell or lease.

Y

Yield: The return on investment from rental income or property appreciation, usually expressed as a percentage of the property's value.

Z

Zoning: Regulations that define how land in specific areas can be used, such as residential, commercial, or industrial purposes.

Understanding these terms will help you navigate the real estate market in India more effectively, whether you are buying, selling, investing, or managing property.

REFERENCES

- **"Home Buying for Dummies" by Eric Tyson and Ray Brown:**
- **"Nolo's Essential Guide to Buying Your First Home" by Ilona Bray:**
- **"The First-Time Homeowner's Survival Guide" by Sid Davis:**
- **"Your First Home: The Proven Path to Home Ownership" by Gary Keller:**
- **"The Millionaire Real Estate Investor" by Gary Keller:**
- **"Rich Dad Poor Dad" by Robert T. Kiyosaki:**
- **"Real Estate Investing for Dummies" by Eric Tyson and Robert S. Griswold.**
- **"Shift: How Top Real Estate Agents Tackle Tough Times" by Gary Keller: 4. Online Resources and Blogs**
- A popular real estate investment community and forum that offers blogs, podcasts, and e-books on various real estate topics. It's an excellent resource for understanding common concerns and questions from first-time buyers.
- **Various Real Estate Articles:** Provides legal advice, tips, and guides on home buying, selling, and renting. The practical advice found here can help add legal context to your book.
- **"REALTOR® Magazine":** Published by the National Association of Realtors, it includes industry news, market trends, and advice for buyers and sellers.
- **"Real Estate Investment Journal":** Covers market analysis and investment strategies that could help you include information on long-term planning and resale considerations.
- **Real Estate Principles and Practices Courses:** Books and materials used in real estate certification courses can be a valuable source for understanding the foundational principles of property buying.

- **Certified Residential Specialist (CRS) Training Materials:** These courses cover advanced topics in real estate sales and market trends, offering deeper insights that could enhance sections on negotiation and market analysis.

- **MagicBricks and 99acres (India-specific):** Real estate portals with insights into property trends, price indexes, and market dynamics in India.

These resources will give you a well-rounded understanding of the topics that matter to first-time homebuyers and real estate investors, helping you craft an informative and practical guide.

SYNOPSIS

Navigating the real estate market as a first-time homebuyer can be overwhelming, but understanding the process can make it manageable and rewarding. This book focus on demystifying the home buying process, providing step-by-step approaches that cover everything from assessing financial readiness to choosing the right home. These guides, which include practical checklists, address common questions and misconceptions first-time buyers have, empowering readers to make informed decisions.

This book offers crucial knowledge about property price trends, location analysis, and financing options tailored to the Indian market. Together, all the chapters highlight the importance of conducting thorough market research to make better property decisions and provide the data necessary to understand market dynamics.

This book underscore the importance of understanding market shifts, adapting strategies to different economic conditions, and setting realistic goals. These insights are essential for navigating India's unique real estate market, which is influenced by a range of factors like location, demand, and economic policies. By educating readers on these aspects, first-time homebuyers can make sound, data-driven decisions.

Financial preparedness is central to the home buying journey. This book offers actionable advice on budgeting, debt management, and saving for a down payment. These books help readers evaluate their financial health, offering strategies for setting savings goals, improving credit scores, and understanding affordability. Knowing how much home one can afford helps in narrowing down options and avoiding potential financial pitfalls.

For those seeking long-term value and investment potential, this book emphasize real estate as a wealth-building tool. These books introduce readers to the basics of property as an appreciating asset and how to think about a home purchase with future investment potential in mind. Moreover, this book contributes by covering essentials on investment property management, financing, and future resale considerations, which can add depth to a first-time buyer's guide.

Legal aspects are equally important and Indian legal platforms on real estate explain the documentation and legal requirements in property transactions. Understanding the paperwork, legal terms, and potential issues that might arise ensures that first-time buyers can protect their investment and approach property transactions confidently.

Through the lens of chapters of this book, it is a comprehensive guide for first-time homebuyers in India and can offer detailed advice on every step—from initial budgeting to final closing. Such a guide would blend the financial, market, legal, and practical insights essential to making informed, empowered decisions in the real estate journey.

www.ingramcontent.com/pod-product-compliance
Lightning Source LLC
Chambersburg PA
CBHW031123130726
47988CB00006B/2200